P9-EEI-516

THE PARABLES OF JESUS

The Storyteller's Companion to the Bible™

Dennis E. Smith and
Michael E. Williams, editors

VOLUME ELEVEN

THE PARABLES OF JESUS

Abingdon Press
Nashville

THE PARABLES OF JESUS

This book is printed on acid-free paper.

Library of Congress Cataloging-in-Publication Data

The Storyteller's companion to the Bible.
Includes indexes.
Contents: v. 1. Genesis—v. 2. Exodus-Joshua—[etc.]—v. 9. Stories about Jesus in the Synoptic Gospels—[etc.]—v. 13. New Testament Women.

1. Bible—Paraphrases, English. 2. Bible—Criticism, interpretation, etc. I. Williams, Michael E. (Michael Edward), 1950-
BS550.2.S764 1991 220.9'505 90-26289

ISBN 0-687-39670-0 (v. 1 : alk. paper)
ISBN 0-687-39671-9 (v. 2 : alk. paper)
ISBN 0-687-39672-7 (v. 3 : alk. paper)
ISBN 0-687-39674-3 (v. 4 : alk. paper)
ISBN 0-687-39675-1 (v. 5 : alk. paper)
ISBN 0-687-00838-7 (v. 6 : alk. paper)
ISBN 0-687-00120-X (v. 7 : alk. paper)
ISBN 0-687-00101-3 (v. 9 : alk. paper)
ISBN 0-687-05585-7 (v. 10 : alk. paper)
ISBN 0-687-06126-1 (v. 11: alk. paper)
ISBN 0-687-08249-8 (v. 12 : alk. paper)
ISBN 0-687-08272-2 (v. 13 : alk. paper)

06 07 08 09 10 11 12 13 14 15—10 9 8 7 6 5 4 3 2 1
MANUFACTURED IN THE UNITED STATES OF AMERICA

Contributors

Bruce J. Ackerson, who holds a Ph.D. in Physics from the University of Nebraska, is Regents Professor of Physics at Oklahoma State University. He writes and tells stories as a hobby and as a means to discover those truths closed to scientific investigation. *(Storyteller)*

Ronald J. Allen is Nettie Sweeney and Hugh Th. Miller Professor of Preaching and New Testament at Christian Theological Seminary, Indianapolis, Indiana, and the author of numerous books and articles on preaching and ministry. *(Commentator)*

Randall Graves is an associate pastor at First United Methodist Church in Bentonville, Arkansas, and an M.Div. student at Phillips Theological Seminary. He is an accomplished author with a special interest in the use of storytelling in preaching and ministry. *(Storyteller)*

Dennis E. Smith, Professor of New Testament at Phillips Theological Seminary, is the primary editor of the New Testament volumes of *The Storyteller's Companion to the Bible*. His research interests range from the social world of early Christianity to the art of storytelling, both ancient and modern. *(Editor of this volume)*

Corinne Stavish is College Professor in Humanities at Lawrence Technological University in Southfield, Michigan, and a professional storyteller who performs at storytelling festivals around the country. She specializes in Jewish folklore and midrashic stories and co-chairs the National Jewish Storytelling Network. *(Storyteller)*

Michael E. Williams, Ph.D. (Northwestern University), a storyteller, writer, and United Methodist Church pastor, is the founding editor of *The Storyteller's Companion to the Bible* and the author of numerous books on storytelling and ministry. *(Founding editor; storyteller for this volume)*

Contents

A Storyteller's Companion

Dennis E. Smith

Jesus was a master storyteller, and his chosen form of story was the parable. Like rabbis of his day and since, if you asked him a question, what you were likely to get in response was a story. As a storyteller, he must have been a charismatic speaker, weaving images that gave people new insights into pressing concerns of their day.

After Jesus' death, his followers preserved many of his stories and passed them down. But when they did so, they saw new meanings in them. Jesus, they felt, spoke not only to people and concerns of his own day but also to new generations and situations. The parables of Jesus were not seen as historical artifacts but as lively words of wisdom appropriate for any generation.

Today we still learn from the parables of Jesus. They still speak with a freshness and power that give us new insights into pressing concerns of our own day. In this volume, we will delve into the master stories of the master storyteller and learn ways in which we can retell those stories for a modern audience.

The Editor

The editor for this volume is Dennis E. Smith. He is Professor of New Testament at Phillips Theological Seminary in Tulsa, Oklahoma, and primary editor for all five of the New Testament volumes in the *Storyteller's Companion to the Bible* series. He combines scholarship in New Testament studies with a strong commitment to the world of storytelling.

The Stories

Each chapter begins with a version of the parable as it is found in one of the Gospels. The featured Gospel version will be the center of the discussion, but other Gospel versions will also be addressed. We have used the Revised English Bible as our translation because it presents us with a fresh telling of the parables in modern English. Rereading the text in a modern translation can help bring the parables to life once more and provide the interpreter with new insights into their meanings.

Comments on the Stories

The commentator for this volume is Ronald J. Allen, who is Nettie Sweeney and Hugh Th. Miller Professor of Preaching and New Testament at Christian Theological Seminary, Indianapolis, Indiana. He is recognized as a leading scholar in the field of preaching and New Testament interpretation and has authored numerous books and articles on preaching and ministry. His analysis provides insights into the multiple ways in which the parables both reflected and addressed the religious, political, and social realities of their day, thus providing a model for how these stories can function in proclamation today.

Retelling the Stories

To help you in developing your own stories, we have provided a sample story with each biblical text. These are intended to serve as models for how a retelling can be done, but they are not expected to exhaust the possibilities in each story. You are encouraged to develop your own retellings according to a format and style that works for you.

The storytellers who have created the stories for this volume have brought a wide range of experiences and perspectives to the task.

Corinne Stavish is College Professor in Humanities at Lawrence Technological University in Southfield, Michigan. She is also a professional storyteller who specializes in Jewish folklore and midrashic stories, co-chairs the National Jewish Storytelling Network, and has performed at festivals across the country, including the National Storytelling Festival and the National Storytelling Conference. Her stories in this volume draw from the Jewish folklore tradition and bring alive the power of the parables to speak universal truths.

Randall Graves is a United Methodist pastor and a senior in the Master of Divinity program at Phillips Theological Seminary. After winning several awards for his creative writing as an undergraduate student, he has begun to apply those skills to the practice of storytelling in ministry. Drawing from his Ozark background, Randy's stories paint pictures of ordinary people in today's world who have a great deal in common with the ordinary people of Jesus' parables.

Bruce J. Ackerson is Regents Professor of Physics at Oklahoma State University in Stillwater, Oklahoma. He is a physics professor with the soul of an artist. He speaks of his storytelling as a hobby and "as a means to discover those truths closed to scientific investigation." His stories provide new ways to understand the parables in order to address contemporary issues.

Michael E. Williams can justly be called the "dean" of biblical storytelling, since he is the founding editor of the *Storyteller's Companion to the Bible* series and a longtime storyteller/pastor. He is a full-time United Methodist

Church pastor who has practiced the art of storytelling in a variety of settings across the nation, ranging from storytelling festivals to local churches. His stories in this volume draw from his experience as a storytelling pastor and address the religious truths at the heart of the parables.

Parallel Stories

Jesus did not tell his stories in a vacuum; he was neither the first nor the only storyteller in his world. He emerged out of a rich storytelling culture. The parallel stories in this volume are provided to bring to our attention the storytelling milieu out of which these parables came. Their purpose is to acquaint us with the ancient world of storytelling so that we can better understand the storyteller's craft and the context in which the parables were originally told and heard. This information will aid the modern storyteller in adapting these parables/stories to fit the sensibilities and experiences of a modern audience.

Most of the parallel stories collected here derive from rabbinic literature. These parallels to the parables of Jesus provide several important perspectives. They illustrate the continuing use of parable form among the rabbis. They preserve examples of some of the same story motifs or plots as those used by Jesus, illustrating how these story forms were part of the culture and continued to be taken up and used by storytellers and Jewish religious teachers over several centuries. They also illustrate how the rabbis continued to struggle with some of the same religious and ethical issues Jesus addressed in his parables.

The parallel stories in this volume were collected by Ron Allen and Dennis Smith.

How to Use This Book

The parables were first told by Jesus and then retold by his followers in subsequent generations to new audiences. By definition they are stories that are intended to be, and indeed must be, retold. Yet are there rules for their retelling?

On the one hand, it is often difficult for people of faith to think that Bible stories can be retold imaginatively. We tend to think of the Bible in rigid terms—as having one, clear, unimpeachable meaning. Yet the plurality of the Gospels themselves leads us to a different conclusion. They present the same parables in different contexts with different meanings, and thus illustrate that it is not only possible but also appropriate to retell the same basic story in different ways.

On the other hand, the possibilities for retelling are not endless; it is possible to tell a story in a form that is not appropriate to the original story. Successful biblical storytelling involves a delicate balance between the meanings inherent in the ancient story, the boundaries of understanding in the modern community within which the story is told, and the imagination of the storyteller who puts it all together. The storyteller must first start with sound methods of interpretation of the biblical text and its meaning in its original context. Then the storyteller's task will be to recast the story into a form that allows it to have meaning in today's context that is consistent with its ancient meaning.

This book is intended to be a resource to promote the telling of Bible stories. But there is an important component that is not present within these pages. That is what you, the reader, bring to the text. Your experiences and understandings are vital to your own creation of viable retellings of the biblical stories. Only in this way can these ancient stories become real and pertinent to the lives of people today.

Reading the Parables

Ronald J. Allen

I sometimes begin my Introduction to the New Testament class by asking the students to write (from memory) a key word, phrase, or image from the first ten passages of the New Testament that come to their minds. Inevitably, parables are at the top of the list. These stories are a part of the soul of the Christian community. A preacher or teacher can often simply refer to a parable and evoke a world of associations in the listeners.

A caution: familiarity with the parables can be deceptive. We can assume that we know the stories when, in fact, we remember selected details. Or, we recall our particular slants on the stories without recollecting the complete story; often, our slants are limited, even distorted. Sometimes we reduce the fullness of the experience of hearing a story to a single point or lesson. In the process, we lose the rich narrative fabric. We sometimes violate the integrity of the parables by reading our own agenda into them. Furthermore, familiarity can be anesthetic. "Oh, the good Samaritan . . . *again*." Yawn. Imaginative storytelling can help keep the parables fresh and provocative. On the other hand, many Boomers and Generation Xers do not know the parables (or other parts of the Bible). Vivid storytelling can help bring the parables to life for these welcome newcomers.

This volume focuses on the parables in Mark, Matthew, and Luke. These stories partake of larger oral-aural and literary phenomena in the ancient world. Awareness of this background can help today's storyteller develop sensitivity to how the parables were heard in the world of the Bible.

Parables in the First Testament

In the First Testament, parables are part of the wide-ranging *mashal* family of speech. The Hebrew term *mashal* means "to be like," "to be similar," or "to compare." *Mashalim* (*mashalim* is the plural form of *mashal*) typically make use of comparison. The following are the most common types of *mashalim*: proverbs (Proverbs 1:1), riddles (Judges 14:1-20), allegories (Isaiah 5:1-7; Ezekiel 17:1-24), and songs of derision (Habakkuk 2:6). Some of these motifs appear in parables in the Gospels. Comparison, for instance, is central to the parable of the mustard seed (Mark 4:30-32; Matthew 13:31-32; Luke 13:18-19).

Nathan's story functions in the tradition of *mashalim* in 2 Samuel 12. King David has Uriah killed so that David can marry Uriah's spouse, Bathsheba.

David's action displeases God, but David shows no remorse. Nathan, a prophet, tells David a story about a poor person who has a beloved ewe lamb. A guest comes to the home of a nearby rich person who has a large flock of lambs. The wealthy person, wanting to preserve the large flock, takes the poor person's beloved ewe lamb in order to serve a meal to the guest. David's anger is kindled greatly against the rich person to the point that David declares that the wealthy one deserves to die. At that moment, Nathan solemnly declares, "You are the man."

David identifies with the poor person in the story. At a crucial juncture in the telling, Nathan gives the interpretation of the story an unexpected twist. David indicts himself.

Several parables in the gospel tradition work on a similar principle: the hearers are drawn into the story through positive identification with the characters, plot, or setting. Then, the story takes an unexpected turn, or receives an unexpected application. The listeners are left in a surprising moment of recognition (cf. the Compassionate Samaritan, Luke 10:25-37).

Parables in Apocalyptic Literature

Apocalyptic literature, which emphasizes visions of the end of time, is not found extensively in the First Testament, but is prominent in Judaism in the time of Jesus and the early church. Apocalyptic writers use the term *parable* to designate several forms of literature that serve a specific purpose: to conceal and disclose the apocalyptic "secret" or "mystery." In this context, "secret" is a technical term. Its content is that the present age is in bondage to Satan and evil. But God will soon initiate a cosmic cataclysm to end Satan's power and establish God's reign (REB: kingdom of heaven) in every arena of life. According to the apocalyptists, this news is hidden from some but is revealed to others. Parables are one of several genres of apocalyptic literature whose purpose is to explain to the initiated the content of the otherwise hidden revelation.

As in the Hebrew Bible, the parables in apocalyptic literature include a variety of forms. Among them are similitude (2 Esdras 8:1-3), narrative with explanation (2 Esdras 4:13-25), vision with interpretation (2 Esdras 4:44-50; *1 Enoch* 37–69), poem (*1 Enoch* 1:2-9), and illustration (*2 Baruch* 22:3-8). Some of the parables are quite lengthy. *First Enoch* 38–44 constitutes a single parable with various parts. While these forms are quite varied, they share a common purpose: they disclose the mysteries (or secrets) of God to the initiated.

In varying degrees, each of the first three Gospels manifests apocalyptic theology. Jesus is the agent through whom God is already beginning the apocalyptic invasion of the world. Two Gospel parables fully exemplify the apocalyptic allegorical genre: the sower and its interpretation (Mark 4:1-20; Matthew 13:1-

23; Luke 8:4-15), and the wheat and the weeds (Matthew 13:24-30, 36-43). Many other Gospel parables, while not thoroughly manifesting apocalyptic forms, resonate with apocalyptic theology; these include the parable of the talents (Matthew 25:14-30; Luke 19:12-27), and the parable of the sheep and the goats (Matthew 25:31-46).

Parables in Rabbinic Literature

The rabbis used *mashalim* in much the same ways as the writers of the First Testament. In addition, the rabbis began to use short narratives, akin to the Gospel parables, for teaching purposes. It is not clear when the rabbis began this practice. The rabbinic literature containing the parables—especially the Talmud and midrashim—was given its present form beginning in the second and third centuries C.E. However, some of the material in these texts appears to be much older. At any rate, rabbis created these stories for specific purposes. They usually illustrate the interpretation of scripture. The most popular characters are kings, natural life, and animals.

Many of the rabbis developed parables with the following structure: (a) a statement of the point to be illustrated; (b) an introductory formula, "It is like . . ."; (c) the story itself, sometimes called the *mashal*; (d) a statement of the application of the story, sometimes called the *nimshal*; and (e) a scriptural citation that demonstrates the truth of the parable and its interpretation. Not all elements are found in each parable. In our explorations of specific parables in the Second Testament, we will find several occurrences of this structure with one exception: the Gospel parables typically omit part (e), the citation from scripture (cf. the Pharisee and the tax collector, Luke 18:9-14). Examples of rabbinic parables are given in various of the "parallel stories" accompanying each chapter.

Our word "parable" is a transliteration of the Greek *parabole*, which means "to cast alongside" or "to throw or set beside." The translators who rendered the Hebrew Bible into Greek used *parabole* to translate the Hebrew *mashal*. The Greek notion of *parabole* was not as fulsome as the Hebrew *mashal*, but many similar elements are present. Aristotle, for instance, uses *parabole* to speak of a story invented by a speaker for a specific purpose, usually to persuade.

Communities in antiquity were accustomed to hearing and processing stories that are similar to the parables in Mark, Matthew, and Luke. Ancient people had an ingrained inclination to listen for a story's particular comparison, twist, or application.

Hearing the Parables Today

Information about how parables were understood in the world of the Bible gives us a background within which to consider the highly influential definition of a parable formulated by C. H. Dodd: "At its simplest the parable is a metaphor or simile drawn from nature or common life, arresting the hearer by its vividness or strangeness, and leaving the mind in sufficient doubt about its precise application to tease it into active thought" (*The Parables of the Kingdom* [New York: Charles Scribner's Sons, 1961], 5). On the one hand, this definition calls attention to a significant characteristic of all the parables in Mark, Matthew, and Luke: each one provokes the listeners to challenging reflection on some aspect of the relationship of God and their everyday worlds. In the most extreme case, parables turn upside down the worldview of the listener. Storytellers can strive to capture this tensive quality.

On the other hand, as we discovered in our review of *mashal* and *parabole* in antiquity, parables sometimes contain a more direct application than might be surmised from Dodd's definition. Indeed, a few of the Gospel parables conclude with a shift from narrative action to a statement that directly addresses the hearers (cf. the parable of the ten young women awaiting the bridegroom, Matthew 25:1-13). This shift may suggest a corresponding shift in the storyteller's style of oral presentation so that the "application" is put directly to the group of hearers.

Each parable, then, is an entity in its own right, and must be interpreted in the light of its particular literary and historical world. Responding to insights from literary and rhetorical criticisms, scholarship today seeks to encounter each parable in its own integrity as a narrative world, and as a part of its larger context in the Gospels.

Consequently, the interpreter seeks to clarify the thoughts, feelings, and other associations that are evoked (or created) by the parable. The storyteller needs to give careful attention to ways that the setting, the characters, and the plot are (or are intended to be) processed by the hearer. The storyteller explores how the parable is heard from different points of view. For instance, one might ask how the Markan version of the parable of the wicked tenants in Mark 12:1-11 is received by (a) the different groups in the immediate audience in the narrative—the disciples of Jesus, the Pharisees, and other leaders in Israel, (b) the Markan community, and (c) today's church.

Some parables appear in more than one Gospel. Yet each Gospel gives the parable its own spin. For instance, the parable of the lost sheep has a very different function in Matthew 18:10-14 than it does in Luke 15:3-7. In the chapters that follow, I will concentrate on one Gospel's version of each parable, but I will often refer to differing nuances in the uses of the parables in the other Gospels. I will also indicate how knowledge of the possible historical situations to which the Gospels were addressed can help us interpret a parable.

An important theme comes into play from recent research into narrative. A story is multivalent; it has more meaning than can be articulated in a single encounter. Further, our life situations as interpreters influence what we are able to receive from a story at a given moment. When my life situation changes, I often see interpretive possibilities that I did not see before. These interrelated phenomena account for occasions when we hear a familiar parable afresh. "Why, I have never before thought of the parable of the pearl of great price in *that* way!" Surprise is a frequent companion of those who hear the parables.

Troubling Aspects of the Parables

Several of the parables have troubling aspects on which preachers, teachers, and storytellers should comment. For example, the parables often present a negative caricature of Jewish people or institutions. Indeed, some interpreters think that occasional parables picture God rejecting the Jewish people in part or in whole (cf. the parable of the wicked tenants, Mark 12:1-12). Over the centuries, some Christians have used such portrayals to claim that God no longer loves all or part of the Jewish people. Indeed, some in the church have used the story to justify anti-Semitism. The storyteller should discourage today's listeners from appropriating the parables in ways that reinforce anti-Judaism or anti-Semitism.

In my judgment, this situation calls the contemporary Christian leader to do four things. First, exegetical honesty demands that such stories should be allowed to make their own points. We need to understand the narrative functions of the negative caricatures of Judaism in the Gospels.

Second, preachers, teachers, and storytellers need to explain the origins of this negative caricature to the congregation. The earliest Christian community was a sect within Judaism; the earliest Christians were Christian Jews. By the time of the writing of the four Gospels (about 70–100 C.E.), tensions developed between Judaism and the Christian community. Most interpreters think that the separation was provoked by controversy regarding the Gentile mission of the church. With differing degrees of intensity, the four Gospel writers created negative portraits of the Pharisees (and several other Jewish groups) and retrojected that caricature into the story of Jesus for the purpose of helping justify the growing separation between Judaism and the Christian movement.

Third, today's Christian leader needs to help the congregation become aware of the heinous effects of this caricature upon the relationships between Christians and Jews. We should critique the negative portrait as historically dishonest and inappropriate to a gospel of universal love and universal justice.

Fourth, when hermeneutically appropriate and when sensitively handled, today's Christian leader may be able, nonetheless, to help the congregation recognize that aspects of the negative qualities of Jewish people and practices represented in caricature in the parables are negative qualities present in today's Christian community. For instance, the Pharisee in Luke's parable of the Pharisee and the tax collector (Luke 18:9-14) sits in the pews of many Christian churches. In order to minimize the suggestion of anti-Judaism when taking this track, the preacher, teacher, or storyteller should emphasize, again and again, the polemical nature of the Gospel portraits.

Many Christians are troubled by another aspect of the parables: the condemnation of some people to eternal fire. For instance, at the end of the parable of the separation of the great catch, the wicked are thrown into "the blazing furnace, where there will be wailing and grinding of teeth" (Matthew 13:50). Poorly informed Christians sometimes distinguish between the vengeful God of the First Testament, who commanded the slaughter of Israel's enemies (and even some within Israel), with the loving God of the Second Testament. But in texts like this one in Matthew, where eternal punishment rather than mere earthly death is the theme, the Second Testament is seen to be every bit as problematic as the First.

The gospel is the news of God's unconditional love for each and all, and God's unremitting call for justice for each and all. Justice, in the gospel context, refers to relationships that express unconditional love. In my view, the painful, eternal condemnation presumed in several of the parables goes against the divine character. The element of eternal condemnation must be critiqued as inappropriate to the gospel.

Do the parables have no value to the contemporary church when they portray judgment befalling certain characters? To the contrary, such parables are stringent reminders of the fact that human actions have consequences. While God may not cast human beings into perpetual fire, unfaithfulness ultimately results in values and practices that eventually cause the community that follows them to collapse. The story functions to motivate people to respond positively to signs of the rule of God. Thus, while such texts contain problematic elements, positive values can result from our encounter with such passages.

Other Christians find it difficult to believe that God will (or can) intervene in history in a blinding, single, cosmic moment as predicted by many Jewish and Christian apocalyptists and as presumed in many of the parables. Contemporary Christians may reason that God is ever present in the world in patient and persistent love. God offers the participants in each moment opportunities for more fully responding to the divine rule. People and other creatures help manifest God's rule by accepting God's invitations; they frustrate God's design by refusing the divine invitations. God's reservoirs of energy are endless. Hence, while God may not wipe out evil in a single blast, God is patiently and perpetually working for a time when love will be all in all. The parables can help us recognize God's presence and purposes in each moment, and can lure us to want to commit ourselves to that presence and purpose. As theologian Clark M. Williamson reminds us, the parables also help us remember that what we do, day to day, matters ultimately because it matters to The One Who Is Ultimate.

Learning to Tell Bible Stories

A Self-Directed Workshop

1. Read the story aloud at least twice. You may choose to read the translation included here or the one you are accustomed to reading. We recommend that you examine at least two translations as you prepare, so you can hear the differences in the way they sound when read aloud.

Do read them *aloud*. Yes, if you are not by yourself, people may give you funny looks, but this really is important. Your ear will hear things about the passage that your eye will miss. Besides, you can't skim when you read aloud. You are forced to take your time, and you might notice aspects of the story that you never saw (or heard) before.

As you read, pay special attention to *where* the story takes place, *when* the story takes place, *who* the characters are, *what* objects are important to the story, and the general *order of events* in the story.

2. Now close your eyes and imagine the story taking place. This is your chance to become a playwright/director or screenwriter/filmmaker because you will experience the story on the stage or screen in your imagination. Enjoy this part of the process. It takes only a few minutes, and the budget is within everybody's reach.

3. Look back at the story briefly to make sure you haven't left out any important people, places, things, or events.

4. Try telling the story. This works better if you have someone to listen (even the family pet will do). You can try speaking aloud to yourself or to an imaginary listener. Afterward ask your listener or yourself what questions arise as a result of this telling. Is the information you need about the people, places, things, or language in the story? Is it appropriate to the age, experiences, and interests of those who will be hearing it? Does the story capture your imagination? One more thing: You don't have to be able to explain the meaning of a story to tell it. In fact, those of the most enduring interest have an element of mystery about them.

5. Read the "Comments on the Story" provided for each passage. Are some of your questions answered there? You may wish also to look at a good Bible dictionary for place names, characters, professions, objects, or worlds that you need to learn more about. *The Interpreter's Dictionary of the Bible* (Nashville: Abingdon Press, 1962; to be superseded by *The New Interpreter's Dictionary*

of the Bible, forthcoming) and *The Anchor Bible Dictionary* (New York: Doubleday, 1992) are the most complete sources for Bible study. A good one-volume source is the *HarperCollins Bible Dictionary* (San Francisco: Harper-SanFrancisco, 1996).

6. Read the "Retelling the Story" section for the passage you are learning to tell. Does it give you any ideas about how you will tell the story? How would you tell it differently? Would you tell it from another character's point of view? How would that make it a different story? Would you transfer it to a modern setting? What places and characters will you choose to correspond to those in the biblical story? Remember, the retellings that are provided are not meant to be told exactly as they are written here. They are to serve as springboards for your imagination as you develop your own telling.

7. Read the "parallel stories" that accompany each passage. These give you insights into the raw materials used by the original storyteller in putting together the biblical story. An appreciation for the "craft" of the ancient storyteller will help you develop your own craft as a storyteller.

8. Once you have the elements of the story in mind and have chosen the approach you are going to take in retelling it, you need to practice, practice, practice. Tell the story aloud ten or twenty or fifty times over a period of several days or weeks. Listen as you tell your story. Revise your telling as you go along. Remember that you are not memorizing a text; you are preparing a living event. Each time you tell the story, it will be a little different, because you will be different (if for no other reason than that you have told the story before).

9. Then "taste and see" that even the stories of God are good—not all sweet, but good and good for us and for those who hunger to hear.

The Seed and the Soils

Jesus compares the imprecision of sowing seed with the imprecision of spreading the word in the human community.

The Story

On another occasion he began to teach by the lakeside. The crowd that gathered round him was so large that he had to get into a boat on the lake and sit there, with the whole crowd on the beach right down to the water's edge. And he taught them many things by parables.

As he taught, he said:

'Listen! A sower went out to sow. And it happened that as he sowed, some of the seed fell along the footpath; and the birds came and ate it up. Some fell on rocky ground, where it had little soil, and it sprouted quickly because it had no depth of earth; but when the sun rose it was scorched, and as it had no root it withered away. Some fell among thistles; and the thistles grew up and choked the corn, and it produced no crop. And some of the seed fell into good soil, where it came up and grew, and produced a crop; and the yield was thirtyfold, sixtyfold, even a hundredfold.' He added, 'If you have ears to hear, then hear.'

When Jesus was alone with the Twelve and his other companions they questioned him about the parables. He answered, 'To you the secret of the kingdom of God has been given; but to those who are outside, everything comes by way of parables, so that (as scripture says) they may look and look, but see nothing; they may listen and listen, but understand nothing; otherwise they might turn to God and be forgiven.'

He went on: 'Do you not understand this parable? How then are you to understand any parable? The sower sows the word. With some the seed falls along the footpath; no sooner have they heard it than Satan comes and carries off the word which has been sown in them. With others the seed falls on rocky ground; as soon as they hear the word, they accept it with joy, but it strikes no root in them; they have no staying-power, and when there is trouble or persecution on account of the word, they quickly lose faith. With others again the seed falls among thistles; they hear the word, but worldly cares and the false glamour of wealth and evil desires of all kinds come in and choke the word, and it proves barren. But there are some with whom the seed is sown on good soil; they accept the word when they hear it, and they bear fruit thirtyfold, sixtyfold, or a hundredfold.'

Comments on the Story

As listeners to the Gospel of Mark, we await Jesus' instruction when he sits in a boat to teach.

"A sower went out to sow." Farmers in the ancient world sowed by broadcasting. Broadcasting was not precise. To ensure that a field was thoroughly planted, the farmer would broadcast the entire field. As this parable indicates, some seed fell on parts of the field that were not well suited for growth.

Some seed fell on the footpath. In Palestine, roads were not well defined. Paths commonly meandered across fields. The surface of the path was hard. Birds could devour the seeds with the convenience of eating from a plate.

Other seed fell on rocky ground. In some places in Palestine, a limestone layer lies just below the surface of the soil. The seed strikes the soil and puts down a root, but the root cannot penetrate the rock. Consequently, the plant scorches and withers.

Still other seed fell among thistles (thorns). The seed began to grow, but the surrounding vegetation made it impossible for the seed to get adequate light and water.

But the seed that fell into the good soil produced abundantly. In the era of the Bible, a tenfold return was adequate. Yields of thirty and sixtyfold were good. A harvest of a hundredfold was remarkable.

After telling the story, Jesus is alone with a group of followers. They do not understand the parables, for they ask Jesus to interpret them (Mark 4:10). Jesus explains that this select group of followers has been given the secret of the rule of God, "but to those who are outside, everything comes by way of parables" (4:11).

The term "secret" (sometimes rendered "mystery") is key. Characteristically, Mark uses "secret" in a technical sense to refer to the secret that the end of the old age is at hand. God is beginning the new world. In this context, a parable provides insight for those who are initiated into the mystery, but it obfuscates those who do not know the secret. One becomes an "insider" by repentance (Mark 1:14-15).

In Mark 4:12, Jesus cites part of Isaiah 6:9-10. According to Mark's interpretation of Isaiah, the secret is given in obscure parables so that some people will not recognize it, and God authorizes this lack of understanding. Those who do not respond to the invitation to repent cannot understand the parables. As Mark soon says, "For those who have will be given more, and those who have not will forfeit even what they have" (Mark 4:25).

Some people in antiquity used the way of thinking represented in Mark 4:10-12 to explain why many of their contemporaries did not recognize or respond to the in-breaking of God's rule. When they did not repent and join the Jesus movement, they were denied understanding. While I cannot subscribe to the viewpoint that God prevents some people from recognizing the dawn of the divine rule, I can appreciate the importance of this way of thinking to Mark. An encounter with Mark's viewpoint might lead today's preacher, teacher, or storyteller to contrast how she or he explains lack of response to Christian witness in the world today.

In the allegorical interpretation that follows (Mark 4:13-20), the Markan Jesus explains the specific content of the mystery contained in the story. The allegory explains later events in the Gospel narrative and in the Markan community.

"The sower sows the word" (Mark 4:14). The "word" is the news that the rule of God is becoming manifest through the life, death, and resurrection of Jesus (Mark 1:45; 2:2).

Satan takes away the word that is sown in those who are on the footpath (Mark 4:15). The Greek phrase "along the footpath" here is the same as "on the way" in Mark 8:27, when Peter correctly identifies Jesus as the Messiah (Christ). Jesus teaches that he must suffer, die, and only then be raised.

Peter rebukes Jesus. Several times in Mark, the term "rebuke" refers to the exorcism of demons (Mark 1:25; 4:39; 9:25). Peter thinks that Jesus is possessed when Jesus speaks of his suffering and death. However, the reader is set straight when Jesus says to Peter, "Get behind me, Satan!" Satan tries to take away the word! Those who deny that the rule of God is coming through the suffering of Jesus operate under the influence of Satan. This criterion was of immense help to the church in Mark's time when some in the community desired a Messiah (and a discipleship) that exulted in triumph to the neglect of suffering (Mark 13:5, 21-23).

Fourth Ezra used the image of sowing in a form like this parable, but in this case the image refers to the idea that few would finally be saved: "[God says] 'The farmer sows many seeds in the ground and plants many plants, but not all the seeds come up safely in due season, nor do all the plants strike root. It is the same in the world of men: not all who are sown will be saved.'

"To that I [Ezra] replied: 'If I have found favour with you, let me speak. The farmer's seed may not come up, because you did not give it rain at the right time, or it may rot because of too much rain; but man, who was fashioned by your hands and called your image because he is made like you, and for whose sake you formed everything, will you really compare him with seed sown by a farmer? Do not be angry with us, Lord; but spare your people and show them pity, for it is your own creation you will be pitying.'" (*4 Ezra* [2 Esdras] 8:41-45 [late first century C.E.]; see also Boring-Berger-Colpe, 91, no. 96)

Other seed fell on the rocky ground. These people receive the word with joy, but they have no root. They cannot endure the trouble or persecution that arises, and they fall away. Evidently, some in the Markan world are persecuted, or fear the threat of persecution (Mark 13:9-13). But if they endure, they will be a part of the new age (Mark 13:13). The seriousness of having insufficient root is revealed in the garden of Gethsemane when the disciples fall away (Mark 14:50). Peter denies Jesus (Mark 14:66-72). Jesus dies almost alone (Mark 15:40-41).

Other seed falls among thistles. These people are choked by the cares of the world, the lure of wealth, and the desire for other things. A rich person asks Jesus what to do to inherit eternal life. Jesus says to sell everything, to give the money to the poor, and to follow Jesus. The rich person goes away grieving because the possessions are more attractive than the rule of God embodied in Jesus (Mark 10:17-22).

Some people are good soil. "They accept the word when they hear it, and they bear fruit thirtyfold, sixtyfold, or a hundredfold" (Mark 4:20).

The parable offers encouragement to a church that is discouraged with the results of its ministry. The story explains why many people are not receptive: they are not good soil. It assures the Christian community of the size and significance of the harvest. The parable also urges us to ask, What kind of soil am I? What do I need to do to become good soil?

The rabbis also stressed the importance of persistence in sowing, both in the field and in life. "*In the morning sow thy seed, and in the evening withhold not thy hand* (Eccl. XI, 6). R. Eliezer and R. Joshua discussed this. R. Eliezer said: If you have sown in the early season, sow in the late season, for you do not know which will be successful, whether the early sowing or the late sowing, as Scripture continues, *For thou knowest not which shall prosper, whether this or that, or whether they both shall be alike good (Ibid.).*" (*Genesis Rabbah* 51:3 [fifth century C.E.]; from Freedman, 2.541)

Matthew uses the parable (Matthew 13:1-23) to introduce the third of five extended teaching discourses in the Gospel (Matthew 13:1-53). Matthew limits the audience of those who are told the purpose of parables to the disciples.

By expanding the quotation from Isaiah, and by eliminating Mark's phrase "in order that" (Mark 4:12), Matthew takes away some of the stringency of Mark's determinism. Matthew further describes the good soil as the person "who hears the word *and understands it*" (my emphasis). Matthean listeners, especially the Christian community, bear some responsibility for responding appropriately.

Luke (Luke 8:4-15) emphasizes the hearer's responsibility to make sense of, and to act upon, the parables (and other aspects of Jesus' ministry). Luke concludes the allegorical interpretation by identifying the good soil as people who "bring a good and honest heart to the hearing of the word, hold it fast, and by their perseverance yield a harvest" (Luke 8:15). The first act in bearing fruit is repentance (Luke 3:8-9). Acts 2:46, which was written by the same author, echoes the phrase "good heart" in Luke 8:15 with the phrase "glad and generous hearts," and thereby implies that participation in the Christian community is a mode of bearing fruit. Such participation requires patient endurance, as is made clear by the death of Jesus, and by the repeated misunderstandings, imprisonments, threats, and martyrdom of Christian witnesses in Acts.

Other factors suggest that, for Luke, the story also functions as an encouragement to share one's possessions with the needy. The parable immediately follows the story of women who financially support Jesus and the disciples (Luke 8:1-3). The echo of Acts 2:42-46 calls to mind the way in which the early church provided financially for one another. The mention of "heart" leads the reader to the parable of the rich fool (Luke 12:13-21), Jesus' exhortation to the disciples to trust in God's providence for their needs (Luke 12:22-31), and the call to sell possessions and give alms (Luke 12:32-33). "For where your treasure is, there will your heart be also" (Luke 12:34).

Retelling the Story

"Listen! A sower went out to sow." (Mark 4:3)

Once there was a mother who gathered her four children around her. "Listen children, I will show you how to make the bread that my mother taught me to make. And, while we make the bread, I will tell you about my parents and the story of how they came to this land. You must know the story."

The four children, who appeared as identical as grains of wheat, gathered around the table. However, although these children looked exactly alike, each was different inside.

The first child, not knowing anything, was silent. The second, immature child, asked, "Why do we need to learn how to bake bread?" The thistly, third child asked, "Why do you think knowing how to make this bread means anything to me?" The fourth, who wanted to know, asked, "How do we make the bread?"

The mother gave each child enough ingredients to make a loaf of bread. The first child mixed the ingredients, but when the flour spilled, dusted it away. The second child did not knead the dough enough, and the bread was lumpy. The third child put in too much flour, and the bread could not rise. The fourth child measured the ingredients carefully, kneaded the dough for a long time, and listened thoroughly to the story. The dough was smooth.

The mother told them about their grandparents, the land they came from, the work they did, the things they valued, their dreams more numerous than the dust of the earth. All the children appeared to be listening to the stories.

"Now," said the mother, "while the bread is baking, tell me what you remember."

The first child responded, "I remember nothing. I didn't hear you."

The second said, "I only remember a little; my mind wandered."

The third said, "I will not remember anything. I heard you, but I did not listen."

The fourth said, "I listened, Mother. I remember. And, when I have children, I will show them how to make the bread and tell the story." *(Corinne Stavish)*

The Seed Growing Secretly

Jesus compares the rule of God with the mystery of a growing seed.

The Story

He said, 'The kingdom of God is like this. A man scatters seed on the ground; he goes to bed at night and gets up in the morning, and meanwhile the seed sprouts and grows—how, he does not know. The ground produces a crop by itself, first the blade, then the ear, then full grain in the ear; but as soon as the crop is ripe, he starts reaping, because harvest time has come.'

Comments on the Story

According to Mark 1:14-15, the permeating theme of the Gospel of Mark is the apocalyptic manifestation of the "rule" (REB: "kingdom") of God. As the Gospel of Mark unfolds, the listeners discover that Jesus is an agent through whom God's invasion of the old world is beginning. In the strict sense, the rule of God is not dawning, for God has been sovereign all along. But God is now taking fresh steps to fully demonstrate the divine rule. According to Mark, while the first stages of the fresh manifestation took place in the earthly ministry of Jesus, the fulfillment of God's promises awaits Jesus' return. A cosmic cataclysm will complete the work of ending the rule of Satan and establishing the divine will in all things (Mark 13:24-27). The church lives in the interim between Jesus' resurrection and his return in glory.

Mark 4:1-25 explains *that* God's reign is showing itself afresh. This passage teaches the listeners how to interpret the parables, and to commit themselves unreservedly to the divine realm. Jesus encourages the disciples to give themselves unreservedly to the dawning of the rule of God, for "the measure you give is the measure you will receive, with something more besides." Those who turn away from God's movement will "forfeit even what they have" (4:24-25). The parable of the seed growing secretly helps the church understand *how* God's rule is coming through Jesus and *why* they can believe it. The story creates an image intended to reinforce the confidence of the hearers in the coming of the full manifestation of the rule of God. The meaning of this parable is communicated as the listeners experience it. The coming of the rule of God is similar to the story in the parable.

A farmer broadcasts seed on the ground. Having just heard the parable of the sower, which stresses the act of sowing, the hearer is prepared to continue that emphasis. The farmer plays an essential role. But the farmer does not cause the seed to grow.

The ground produces the crop of its own energy. In only a few deft words, the parable causes us to envision the phases of growth. We see the tiny green blade poke its head through the soil. The stalk grows, and soon we see the ear. The preceding parable and its interpretation (Mark 4:1-9, 13-20) cause us to remember that organic development is not always unrelenting progress. Complications (such as thorns that choke the little plants) can retard growth, and even reverse it. Struggle is a part of growth, especially the manifestation of the rule of God.

Mark uses the word "of itself" (Greek *automatē*, from which we get our word "automatic") to describe the process by which the earth brings forth its crop (4:28). This term occurs in the Septuagint (the Greek translation of the First Testament) in Leviticus 25:5 to refer to the growth that takes place in the sabbatical year, and in Leviticus 25:11 to refer to growth in the Jubilee year. Those plants appear in seasons of grace: they sprout and grow without any human effort. In Joshua 6:5, God causes the walls of the city of Jericho to fall of themselves before the Israelites. In retelling the story of the exodus, the Wisdom of Solomon describes a terrifying light shining on the Egyptians

> In *Fourth Ezra,* the giving of the law is compared with the sowing of seed in the hearts of humankind: "Lord, you showed yourself to our fathers in the wilderness at the time of the exodus from Egypt, when they were travelling through a barren waste where no one ever trod, and you said, 'Hear me, Israel, listen to my words, you descendants of Jacob: this is my law, which I am sowing among you to bear fruit and to bring you everlasting glory.' But our fathers, though they received the law, did not observe it; they disobeyed its commandments. Not that the fruit of the law perished—that was impossible, for it was yours; rather, those who received it perished, because they failed to keep safe the seed that had been sown in them. Now the usual way of things is that when seed is put into the earth, or a ship on the sea, or food or drink into a jar, then if the seed, or the ship, or the contents of the jar should be destroyed, what held or contained them does not perish along with them. But with us sinners it is different: destruction will come upon us, the recipients of the law, and upon our hearts, the vessel that held the law. The law itself is not destroyed; it survives in all its glory." (*4 Ezra* [2 Esdras] 9:29-37 [late first century C.E.]; see also Boring-Berger-Colpe, 91, no. 97)

"of no human making." The Egyptians soon "collapsed in terror" (17:6-10). In Acts 12:10, God frees the disciples from prison when the prison doors open of themselves. This term, then, prompts the hearer to realize that God's gracious, liberating power is at work.

At last we see the mature grain in the ear. The process of growth takes place slowly but inexorably. When the grain is ripe, the farmer immediately comes with the sickle and harvests the crop. Several Jewish writers used the harvest motif to speak of the fulfillment of God's purposes (Isaiah 27:12-13; 2 Esdras 4:28ff.; 9:17, 31; *2 Baruch* 70:2ff). Mark specifically echoes the similar usage in Joel 3:13. The larger context of Joel 3:9-17 announces divine comfort for suffering Israel (3:14-17) and violent destruction for Israel's enemies (3:9-13). The harvest is a time of rejoicing for those who repent and welcome the incoming of the rule of God. But for those who resist, it is an occasion for judgment.

The mention of seed and growth also calls to mind Genesis 1:11-12. The process of growth is guaranteed by God, who created seeds to grow and mature. God promised Noah that seedtime and harvest would continue as long as the earth lasts (Genesis 8:22). The continuation of the fruitfulness of the earth through the long years of human brokenness is a sign of divine faithfulness. Hence, people can trust the process by which the rule of God is coming. As God could be trusted in the first creation, so God will prove trustworthy for the new creation.

The situation of Mark's community is similar to the situation in the parable. Why should Christians continue to plant the hope for a new world in the face of the ongoing pain and evil in the present age? We can continue to believe that a new creation is growing because the God who created once has promised to recreate. The community cannot know the day or the hour of the harvest (Mark 13:32-37). Indeed, in the midst of the suffering of the world, signs of struggle may be more prominent than signs of the coming of God. Like the seed germinating invisibly below the surface of the soil, the rule of God is sometimes at work below the surface of current events. We patiently continue our planting and waiting. For the growth cannot be stopped, even if it does not come quickly.

The echo from Joel reminds the listening community that the stakes are high. Those who continue steadfastly will join the full grain in the basket. Those who turn away fall under judgment.

Retelling the Story

"... the seed sprouts and grows—how, he does not know." (Mark 4:27b)

The stranger appeared at the door, tired and hungry. The old woman invited him in for lunch and made him a sandwich with thick slices of bread.

"Thank you, ma'am," said the stranger. "The bread was delicious."

"Don't thank me," the woman replied. "I bought the bread from the grocer. Thank him."

So, the stranger found the grocer and said, "Thank you for the delicious bread I ate at the woman's house today."

"Oh, don't thank me," said the grocer. "I bought the bread from the baker across the street. She's the best baker in town. It's her you should thank."

So the stranger walked to the bakeshop and went in to speak with the baker.

"Thank you for the delicious bread I ate at the woman's house today," he said. "The grocer said that you make the best bread in town."

"Oh, don't thank me," said the baker. "What makes my bread so delicious is the fine flour I use. The miller grinds the wheat carefully and thoroughly. It's the miller you should thank."

So the stranger walked further through the town until he came to the miller's. "Thank you for the delicious bread I ate at the woman's house today," he said. "The baker said that it's because of the way you grind the wheat that makes the bread so delicious."

"Oh, don't thank me," said the miller. "I do grind the wheat well, but the farmer I get the wheat from grows the best wheat around. He's the one you should thank."

So the stranger walked much further, until he came to the farm the miller directed him to. He saw the farmer and his family in the fields, harvesting the wheat. "Thank you for the delicious bread I ate at the woman's house today," he said. "The miller told me that your wheat was the finest and that's why the bread is so delicious."

"Oh, don't thank me," said the farmer.

"Then who?" asked the stranger.

"Help us finish harvesting this wheat; stay for supper and I will show you," said the farmer.

So the stranger spent the afternoon with the farmer and his family, working in the fields. And that evening he gathered with them around their dinner table. He joined the circle of hands as the farmer blessed the bread and said, "Praised be Thou oh Lord our God, who brings forth the bread of the earth." *(Corinne Stavish)*

The Mustard Seed

The rule of God is like a tiny mustard seed that grows into a giant bush.

The Story

He said, 'How shall we picture the kingdom of God, or what parable shall we use to describe it? It is like a mustard seed; when sown in the ground it is smaller than any other seed, but once sown, it springs up and grows taller than any other plant, and forms branches so large that birds can roost in its shade.'

Comments on the Story

Many of the comments from our previous encounter with the parable of the seed growing secretly (Mark 4:26-29) can be adapted to the parable of the mustard seed. This story, too, is a comparison with the rule of God. The parable of the mustard seed also draws upon agricultural imagery familiar to first-century auditors. It invokes the motif of growth.

As listeners, our first impression is of the mustard seed, which the story calls "smaller than any other seed." While this identification is not strictly true (the orchid seed is smaller), the narrator is directly preparing us for the contrast between the tiny seed and the large bush. The mustard plant reaches a minimum of four feet in height, and can grow to eight or twelve feet. In antiquity, much as today, mustard was used as a condiment. It could transform a bland food into a spicy delicacy. It was also used as a medicine for problems ranging from snake bites to stomach troubles and sneezing. The hearer thus thinks of the rule of God as a healing realm. The mustard plant spread so rapidly that it was seldom planted in a garden. The energetic growth of the mustard plant leads the listener to imagine similar energy in the dominion of God.

The experience of contrast is central to the meaning of the story. We see the tiny seed, and then we are surprised by the giant bush that results. The beginning of the cosmic manifestation of God's rule is like the mustard seed: so tiny as to be overlooked. What could be less auspicious than a crucified carpenter who traveled around Palestine preaching, teaching, and working an occasional miracle? What could be less impressive than the ragged church Jesus left behind to claim that he was raised from the dead and that he would return again in heavenly power and glory?

In the Markan version of the parable, the fully grown mustard plant is described only as a shrub. Both Matthew and Luke speak of it as a tree. Scholars debate whether an essential difference results from the divergence between shrub and tree.

According to one interpretation, the shrub of Mark is a direct contrast to certain trees in the Hebrew Bible. In Ezekiel 31:1-18 and in Daniel 4:10-12, 20-27, large trees represent powerful, idolatrous empires that are destroyed. Some scholars contend that Mark deliberately avoids calling the mustard plant a "tree" in order to indicate that the rule of God appears to be less than it actually is. Egypt, Babylon, and other haughty empires, full of pride, called themselves trees, but they were cut down. Under divine impulse, the humble mustard plant will become greater than the cedars of Lebanon. Mark's use of the term "shrub" is thus seen as a critique of all earthly pretensions to power.

The philosopher Seneca also made use of the image of the small seed from which a great plant grows: "Words should be scattered like seed; no matter how small the seed may be, if it has once found favorable ground, it unfolds its strength and from an insignificant thing spreads to its greatest growth. Reason grows in the same way; it is not large to the outward view, but increases as it does its work. Few words are spoken; but if the mind has truly caught them, they come into their strength and spring up. Yes, precepts and seeds have the same quality; they produce much, and yet they are slight things." (Seneca, *Epistles,* "Letter to Lucilius" 4.38.2 [first century C.E.]; from Boring-Berger-Colpe, 94, no. 101)

While this interpretation is attractive, I think it unlikely. Why would Matthew and Luke replace such an association with "tree"? A plant twelve feet high can qualify, at least figuratively, as a tree. Furthermore, trees can function positively in Hebrew tradition. In Ezekiel 17:22-24, God describes the restoration of fallen Israel as taking a sprig "from the lofty crown of the cedar" and planting it. Large, well-watered trees can represent God's providential care (Psalm 104:12, 16-17). The motif of contrast again comes into play: the future, cosmic tree is continuous with the tiny mustard seed.

The picture of the birds nesting on the large branches creates an image of trust and security in the hearer. When we identify with God's coming rule, we feel similarly.

Further, in Ezekiel 17:23; 31:5-6; and Daniel 4:12, birds nesting in branches bespeak the diverse inhabitants of the dominions represented by the trees. In *1 Enoch* 90:2-3, 30-37 and in *Joseph and Aseneth* 15:7, birds specifically portray Gentiles. The rule of God is cosmic in scope and international in population.

Today's preacher or teacher occasionally claims that the presence of Gentiles in the cosmic dominion of God offends Jewish exclusivism. Quite the contrary. At its best, Judaism understands its witness to be for the sake of the whole human family and the larger natural world (as in Genesis 12:1-3; Isaiah 42:1-9). Indeed, the Jewish community looks forward to the day when God will reunite the whole human family (Isaiah 2:2-4; 25:6-8; 44:5; 60:4-7; Jeremiah 16:19-20; Micah 4:1-3; Zechariah 8:20-23; *1 Enoch* 90:13, 37-38; 91:14; *Sibylline Oracles* 3:767-795; Tobit 13:6). Early Christians believed that the knowledge of God that had been enjoyed by Israel since Abraham and Sarah was extended to Gentiles through Jesus Christ. The presence of the birds in the tree in the parables indicates that the rule of God includes the great Gentile ingathering. The purpose of the Markan church is to witness among Gentiles (Mark 13:10). Since the birds in Ezekiel 31 and Daniel 4 are subjects of pagan empires, their appearance in Mark's tree suggests that in the rule of God, even idolaters can be transformed.

Matthew's version of the parable of the mustard seed (13:31-32) is not substantially different from Mark's. Matthew places the parable in a collection of parables where its function is similar to its role in Mark 4: it provides information about the rule of God.

Luke 13:18-19 abbreviates the story. Luke also changes the place of planting from the "ground" to a garden. As he does elsewhere, Luke probably changes this detail in order to make the story more understandable to people who live in cities and who might have an herb garden. Luke also puts the parable in a new context. In 12:49-59, Jesus announces that the time of judgment is coming. In 13:1-9, Jesus stresses that all who do not repent will perish under judgment. In 13:10-17, Jesus embodies the rule of God by healing a bent-over woman in a synagogue on the sabbath. The leader of the synagogue upbraids Jesus for healing on the sabbath. As a commentary on the incident, Jesus then tells the parables of the mustard seed and the leaven. The parables remind the listeners that while their witness to the divine rule may bring them into conflict with authorities, the reign of God is inevitably coming. When the rule of God is fully manifest, those who do not repent will perish. Those who welcome the coming of God in events such as the healing of the woman will nest in the tree of God's rule.

According to the rabbis, the mustard seed was proverbially fruitful. "It was taught: R. Joseph related: It once happened to a man at Shihin to whom his father had left three twigs of mustard that one of these split and was found to contain nine kab of mustard, and its timber sufficed to cover a potter's hut." (*b. Ketubbot* 111b [ca. fourth century C.E.]; from Epstein, 13.721)

Retelling the Story

> " . . . once sown, it springs up and grows taller than any other plant, and forms branches so large that birds can roost in its shade." (Mark 4:32)

They walked together near the olive trees at the border hand in hand, grandmother and grandson. When they stopped to rest, the little boy looked up at his grandmother and said, "People say that here the olives grow bigger and more tasty than anywhere in the land and that the blossoms are the most beautiful on these olive trees. Why is that, Grandma?" "Well, as with most important things, there's a reason," his grandmother replied. "And, I've been waiting for you to be old enough to tell you this story. You see, it is a true story. In fact, the story is about my father, who told it to me when I was about your age and he had brought me here for the first time.

"When my father was a little boy, Israel was not yet a state, but the Arabs and the Jews were enemies and my father was not allowed to play down here near the border between the Jewish village and the Arab village. His parents forbade him to go near the Arab village, and my father was a good boy, so he listened. But one day, I guess perhaps his head was in the clouds and his mind journeyed away. He crossed from his side of the village to the Arab side and before he realized it, my father was surrounded by the older Arab boys, who began to tease and taunt him. Because he was very small and not sure of the language and afraid of both the boys and what his parents would say if they knew, my father began to cry. But the boys, they began to shout and continued to taunt him.

"And then through the crowd, my father heard someone yelling at the older boys to leave my father alone. The voice belonged to a small Arab boy and amazingly, the older boys listened to that little boy, and they stopped taunting my father. Now perhaps the older boys were tired, or perhaps they had achieved what they wanted, which was to get my father to cry, but whatever the reason, they left and my father turned to the small Arab boy who had rescued him. The boy was wiry and frail, but feisty. He had hair as black as the raven's wing and dazzling black eyes that glistened and gleamed in the sunlight. The two boys looked at one another . . . and they smiled.

"They played all that day, the games that all children play. They acted out scenes and adventures from their individual and mutual heritage. They re-created the heroes from their own cultures, and they told each other new words and shared games from their separate cultures. At day's end, the Arab boy asked my father to return the next day and my father promised. And, he came back and he played.

"He returned the day after that and the day after that until, eventually, his mother asked him why he didn't play with his friends on his street, wanting to know where he went each day. My father was an honest boy, so he told her. She grew alarmed and told his father, and together they made him promise never to return to the Arab village, ever. My father did promise that he would never go back, but he broke that promise only once for he was a good boy. But, he felt he had to go back and tell his friend why he could never return to play again. His friend understood. He knew his parents would never allow him to go to the Jewish village if the situation were reversed. The boys played all that day. Before they said good-bye, they took the pits from the olives they had with lunch, and in a gesture more symbolic than practical, with intuitiveness beyond their years, they sowed the seeds along the border, watered the earth, and then said good-bye forever. From those seeds these olive trees grew more beautiful, more fragrant and larger than anywhere in the land, a testimony to that forbidden friendship."

When his grandmother stopped talking, the boy thanked her for sharing the story and then he told her that he would like to come back often to this place that he now called his grandfather's olive grove. They rose together to leave. Hearing a noise, the boy turned and saw a small Arab boy who was wiry and frail, but feisty, with hair as black as the raven's wing, and dazzling black eyes that glistened and gleamed in the sunlight. The two boys looked at one another . . . and they smiled. *(Corinne Stavish)*

MARK 12:1-12 (MATTHEW 21:33-46; LUKE 20:9-19)

The Wicked Tenants in the Vineyard

A parable of a workers' revolt at a vineyard provides a theological interpretation of the death of Jesus and the fall of the temple.

The Story

He went on to speak to them in parables: 'A man planted a vineyard and put a wall round it, hewed out a winepress, and built a watchtower; then he let it out to vine-growers and went abroad. When the season came, he sent a servant to the tenants to collect from them his share of the produce. But they seized him, thrashed him, and sent him away empty-handed. Again, he sent them another servant, whom they beat about the head and treated outrageously, and then another, whom they killed. He sent many others and they thrashed some and killed the rest. He had now no one left to send except his beloved son, and in the end he sent him. "They will respect my son," he said; but the tenants said to one another, "This is the heir; come on, let us kill him, and the inheritance will be ours." So they seized him and killed him, and flung his body out of the vineyard. What will the owner of the vineyard do? He will come and put the tenants to death and give the vineyard to others.

'Have you never read this text: "The stone which the builders rejected has become the main corner-stone. This is the Lord's doing, and it is wonderful in our eyes"?'

They saw that the parable was aimed at them and wanted to arrest him; but they were afraid of the people, so they left him alone and went away.

Comments on the Story

In Mark, the setting is important for hearing the parable of the wicked tenants. Mark presumes that the reader knows that the temple in Jerusalem—a prominent symbol of God's promises and power—had already been destroyed by the Romans in 70 C.E. Mark also gradually presents a case to persuade the listener to recognize that Satan and the demons have entered into those leaders in Israel who object to Jesus and his ministry (Mark 1:12-13; 3:19-30; 8:11-13; 14:43; 14:53-65; 15:13; 15:31).

The narrative atmosphere within which we hear this parable is tense with conflict. According to Mark 12:1, Jesus tells the story to his opponents. At one level Jesus confronts them with the meaning and consequences of their behavior.

At another level, the parable offers the Markan listener a theological interpretation of the death of Jesus and the fall of the temple.

A landowner plants a vineyard. A vineyard is to give produce (Mark 12:2). The Greek for "produce" is *karpos*, a term frequently translated "fruit." In Mark 4:20, a word from the *karpos* family is a figure of speech for personal and communal life that exhibits God's purposes. This meaning is typical of usages in Jewish and early Christian literature (Proverbs 1:31; Isaiah 3:10; Jeremiah 17:10; Hosea 10:13; Amos 6:12; Wisdom 3:15; Ecclesiasticus 14:15; 2 Esdras 9:31-32; Matthew 3:10; 7:15-20; Romans 7:5).

The mention of the vineyard immediately causes the listener to think of Israel, for several passages in Jewish literature describe Israel as a vineyard. The call of Israel is to bear the fruit of God's will. This allusion immediately creates a tension for the hearer, for some of the images of Israel as a vineyard are positive, and others are negative. In Isaiah 5:1-7, for instance, God plants Israel as a vineyard. But, alas, the vines yield wild grapes, prompting the vineyard owner to make it a waste. Other passages similarly reflect on Israel as a spoiled vine (for example, Hosea 10:1; Jeremiah 2:20-25; Ezekiel 15:1-8; 19:10-14; Psalm 80:8-13). However, in Isaiah 65:8-16, Israel's faithful remnant is likened to a cluster of grapes. The spouse of a faithful Israelite is like a fruitful vine (Psalm 128:3). An apocalyptic Jewish writing looks forward to the eschatological vineyard in which each

The rabbis tell a similar story in which the unfaithful tenants are Gentiles: "*For the portion of the Lord is His people* (32:9): A parable: A king had a field which he leased to tenants. When the tenants began to steal from it, he took it away from them and leased it to their children. When the children began to act worse than their fathers, he took it away from them and gave it to (the original tenants') grandchildren. When these too became worse than their predecessors, a son was born to him. He then said to the grandchildren, 'Leave my property. You may not remain therein. Give me back my portion, so that I may repossess it.' Thus also, when our father Abraham came into the world, unworthy (descendants) issued from him, Ishmael and all of Keturah's children. When Isaac came into the world, unworthy (descendants) issued from him, Esau and all the princes of Edom, and they became worse than their predecessors. When Jacob came into the world, he did not produce unworthy (descendants), rather all his children were worthy, as it said, *And Jacob was a perfect man, dwelling in tents* (Gen. 25:27). When did God repossess His portion? Beginning with Jacob, as it is said, *For the portion of the Lord is His people, Jacob the lot of His inheritance* (32:9), and, *For the Lord hath chosen Jacob unto Himself* (Ps. 135:4)." (*Sifre to Deuteronomy* 32:9 [third century C.E.]; from Hammer, 318; see also Boring-Berger-Colpe, 124, no. 157)

vine will produce 1,000 branches. Each branch will produce 1,000 grapes. Each grape will yield 120 gallons of wine (*2 Baruch* 29:5). At the beginning then, the listener puzzles, "What kind of vineyard is the one in the parable?"

The lifelike details of the vineyard in Mark 12:1 are drawn from Isaiah 5:2 (thereby giving the auditor a preview of the subsequent drift of the parable and casting a foreboding shadow). They speak of a well-prepared vineyard. A good vineyard would have a wall (or a hedge) to protect the vineyard from wild animals. The wine press is a pit in which people would tread the grapes with their feet. The tower provides shelter for the workers and gives them a good vantage point for spotting jackals and other predators.

The landowner lets out the vineyard to vine-growers and goes abroad. Israel's leaders are compared to the tenants.

The vineyard owner sends a series of servants to collect the owner's share of produce from the vineyard. Jewish tradition sometimes refers to the prophets as servants of God (Jeremiah 7:25; 25:4; Amos 3:7; Zechariah 1:6; *2 Baruch* 2:20, 24). However, the tenants reject each servant. They seize, thrash, and send the first servant away empty-handed. The second servant they beat about the head and treat outrageously. The tenants kill the third servant, and they do likewise to other messengers. With these descriptions Mark evokes memories of Israel rejecting God's envoys (as in 1 Kings 18:12-13; 22:24; Jeremiah 26:20-23; 2 Chronicles 24:20-22; 36:15-16; Nehemiah 9:26).

In the end, the vineyard owner decides to send the "beloved son." The Greek expression for "in the end" in apocalyptic literature often signals events that are a part of the transition between the two ages. Mark has already used the term "beloved son" at the baptism (1:11) and transfiguration (9:7) to describe Jesus. We hear the vineyard owner's profound yearning for the tenants when, despite their previous behavior, the owner hopes that they will welcome this last messenger: "They will respect my son."

To the contrary, when the tenants see the beloved son, they plot to kill him in order for the vineyard to become their inheritance. The expression "Come on, let us kill him" is from the story of Joseph in Genesis 37:20, thus comparing the tenants to the brothers who sought Joseph's end.

In a chilling climax, the owner of the vineyard "puts the tenants to death." The phrase "puts to death" translates a Greek term (*apollumi*) that sometimes refers to the destruction of evil as a result of the apocalyptic cataclysm (see Matthew 10:28; Luke 17:27-30; 1 Corinthians 1:18; 2 Thessalonians 2:10). The hearer knows that God will destroy Satan, the demons, and their orbs of power (1:24; 3:19-27). An irony, of course, is that the Jewish leaders have tried to destroy Jesus (as in 3:6; 11:18). According to Mark, the scribes, priests, and kindred spirits—and their destroyed temple—have no more authority.

The owner then gives the vineyard to others. The vineyard (the community that bears fruit for God) is intact, but the current tenants have been thrown out, and the vineyard is under new management. The parable is thus not a wholesale condemnation of Israel; rather, the story condemns Israel's leaders (12:12). The promises and purposes of God for the vineyard are now in the hands of Jesus and the church.

This point is underscored by the *nimshal*, or application of the story, in 12:10-11. Jesus quotes Psalm 118:22-23, a text frequently cited in early Christian literature (see, for example, Acts 4:11; Romans 9:32-33; Ephesians 2:20; 1 Peter 2:7). While the language shifts from agriculture to architecture, the point is clear: God appoints Jesus and his followers as new authorities in the vineyard. They are to help the vineyard bear fruit as the old age dies and the new one is born.

Another theme may be at work in the hearer's imagination. Psalm 118:19-29 is a liturgy used when entering the temple to give thanks for deliverance from enemies. When Mark was written, the old temple was in ruins. The first-century listener would know that the curtain of the temple that was torn from top to bottom at Jesus' death (15:38) was embroidered with sun, moon, and stars. In the light of Mark 13:24-27, this hearer would understand the destruction of the temple as a key event in the destruction of the old world. Of course, the temple was actually destroyed by the Romans, but in Mark's view it was condemned by God (15:22-38). However, in the parable the vineyard is still a mode of contact with the divine.

Matthew inserts the parable of the two children in the vineyard (Matthew 21:28-32) between the conflict over Jesus' authority and the parable of the wicked tenants (21:33-46). The story of the two children in the vineyard depicts the inversion of two children: one begins faithfully to work in the vineyard, but ends unfaithfully, while the other begins by not working in the vineyard, but ends by faithfully doing so. The first son should follow the advice of John the Baptist (3:7-10) and Jesus (7:17-20; 12:33-37), and repent, and bear the fruit of the rule of God (21:43). The second child bears such fruit. This setting prepares us for the inversion that takes place in the parable of the wicked tenants in which the tenants are cast out of the vineyard.

Matthew intensifies the end of the parable. In 21:41 he describes the landowner inflicting a miserable death upon the tenants and he adds an explicit reference to the "harvest" with its apocalyptic undertones. He also says explicitly that participation in the rule of God is now categorically denied to those who do not recognize the legitimacy of the church's mission. They will be forever crushed (21:43-44).

Matthew adds an allusion to the stones of Isaiah 8:14 and Daniel 2:44 to Matthew 21:44. In Daniel, the dominion of God will crush all other dominions. In Isaiah, God's action for judgment and deliverance is a stone that can either become a sanctuary or a stumbling block, depending upon the community's response. The allusion thus encourages the listeners not to stumble.

Whereas Jesus tells the parable directly to the Jewish leaders in Matthew and Mark, in Luke he tells the story to a much larger group of people. The leaders are present, and they overhear the parable. They are drawn into the story and are shocked to discover that it is about them. Could the storyteller create such a setting and use for today's listeners?

Luke takes away a bit of the criticism of the Jewish leaders by softening the description of how the tenants treated the earlier servants (20:10b-11) and by having them kill only the beloved son (20:12-14). At the end of the pericope, Luke also defuses some of the leaders' reaction to Jesus by saying that they wanted only to "lay hands on him." These changes are consistent with the fact that Luke is somewhat more sympathetic to Jewish leaders than Mark and even Matthew. However, the passage is still stringent as the crowd is stung to discover that some of them will fall under destruction (20:19).

The story asks the listeners, "What kind of fruit are we bearing?" And the story cautions the church to be critically reflective on its leadership. An office may give power to its holder, but an office does not necessarily endow its holder with wisdom.

Retelling the Story

> "When the season came, he sent a servant to the tenants to collect from them his share of the produce." (Mark 12:2)

An emperor was leading his men to war. As they traveled through the forest, he saw an old man planting saplings. The emperor asked the old man, "What kind of saplings are you planting?"

"Figs. These saplings will grow to be fig trees."

"How long will that take?" asked the emperor.

"Three years," replied the aged man.

"And, tell me, how old are you? Your withered skin, frail form, and long beard testify to advanced years."

"You observe well, Your Majesty," said the old man. "I am over one hundred years old!"

The astonished emperor laughed heartily at the old man: "Over a hundred years old? Why would one so ancient plant trees that you surely will never see bear fruit?"

"My dear emperor," replied the old man, "I have spent my life planting and harvesting. I have invested my life in the soil. If I am blessed by God with more years, then I will live to see these trees bear fruit. If not, it will not matter, for my children and their children and their children's children shall eat of these trees. You see, my forefathers planted for me. I in turn will plant for my descendants."

"Old one," said the emperor smiling, "if you are living when these trees bear fruit, come to the palace with the figs."

The emperor remained at war for three years. Upon his return, his advisor informed him that an old man was waiting to see him. The emperor entered his throne room to see the old man from the forest standing behind a large basket of figs. The ancient one smiled joyfully, and the emperor matched his smile, while tasting the fruit.

"Ah, delicious, perfectly ripened," declared the emperor. "Empty your basket. Leave the figs with me." When the basket was empty, the emperor filled it with gold. The old man thanked the emperor and left to share his new wealth with those in need.

When word spread that the emperor was giving gold for fruit, many people started to bring baskets of fruit to the emperor. They were all turned away from the palace, and by order of the emperor, pelted with their own offerings. The emperor explained: "It was not for the fruit that I filled the old man's basket with gold, but rather for his honest labor, his faith in the future, and his commitment to the generations to come." *(Corinne Stavish)*

The Wheat and the Darnel

A story about good seed and bad seed growing together but separated at harvest becomes an allegory about the consummation of history.

The Story

Here is another parable he gave them: 'The kingdom of Heaven is like this. A man sowed his field with good seed; but while everyone was asleep his enemy came, sowed darnel among the wheat, and made off. When the corn sprouted and began to fill out, the darnel could be seen among it. The farmer's men went to their master and said, "Sir, was it not good seed that you sowed in your field? So where has the darnel come from?" "This is an enemy's doing," he replied. "Well then," they said, "shall we go and gather the darnel?" "No," he answered; "in gathering it you might pull up the wheat at the same time. Let them both grow together till harvest; and at harvest time I will tell the reapers, 'Gather the darnel first, and tie it in bundles for burning; then collect the wheat into my barn.'"'

[Matthew then inserts the parables of the mustard seed and the yeast and an explanation of the meaning of parables.]

Then he sent the people away, and went into the house, where his disciples came to him and said, 'Explain to us the parable of the darnel in the field.' He replied, 'The sower of the good seed is the Son of Man. The field is the world; the good seed stands for the children of the Kingdom, the darnel for the children of the evil one, and the enemy who sowed the darnel is the devil. The harvest is the end of time, and the reapers are angels. As the darnel is gathered up and burnt, so at the end of time the Son of Man will send his angels, who will gather out of his kingdom every cause of sin, and all whose deeds are evil; these will be thrown into the blazing furnace, where there will be wailing and grinding of teeth. Then the righteous will shine like the sun in the kingdom of their Father. If you have ears, then hear.'

Comments on the Story

Matthew 13 is the third of five teaching discourses in the first Gospel, and consists of a series of parables and statements about the meaning of the parables. The chapter is a *catena*, a rhetorical device in which the rabbis would string together one story after another on a common theme. The stories are related in stairstep fashion, each narrative amplifying the preceding one with a new piece of information, or a slightly different perspective, or fresh emotional force. The effect of a catena is cumulative.

In chapter 13, the catena instructs the church on the nature of the rule of God, on the rejection of that rule by some Jewish leaders and by some in the church, and on responding to it. The parable of the sower (Matthew 13:3-9) begins the catena. The disciples ask for its interpretation. Jesus speaks in parables to disclose the previously hidden rule of God to the in-crowd of the disciples (vv. 10-17). The allegorical interpretation of the parable compares those who hear the word of the reign of God to the soils, and climaxes with the harvest at the end of history (Matthew 13:18-23). The parable of the wheat and the darnel explains that the harvest will be a time of judgment in which some are gathered into the barn but others are condemned. The parables of the mustard seed and yeast (13:31-33) fortify the reader's confidence that the rule of God is coming. The allegorical interpretation of the parable of the wheat and the darnel explains the ambiguous nature of the world (and the church) while the mustard seed is growing and the leaven is working. A great moment of clarification will come at the judgment and the end of history. At that time, those who are darnel will be burned, and those who are wheat will join God forever in splendor (13:36-43). The parables of the treasure hidden in the field and the pearl of great value help the listener know how to avoid the furnace of fire and to shine like the sun with God. When they see the rule of God, people should respond to it with all that they have (13:44-46). The parable of the separation of the fish climaxes the catena by underscoring the consequences of the great judgment (13:47-50). The church's mission is to cast the net. Both good fish and bad will respond. At the end of history, God will save the good fish, but will throw the bad fish into the fire.

> *Fourth Ezra* also spoke of the end time as a harvest of evil seed and good seed: "He answered: 'If you survive, you will see; if you live long enough, you will marvel. For this present age is passing away; it is full of sorrow and weakness, too full to grasp what is promised in due time for the godly. The evil about which you ask me has been sown, but the time for reaping is not yet. Until the crop of evil has been reaped as well as sown, until the ground where it was sown has vanished, there will be no room for the field where the good is sown. A grain of the evil seed was sown in the heart of Adam from the first; how much godlessness has it produced already! How much more will it produce before the harvest! Reckon this up: if one grain of evil seed has produced so great a crop of godlessness, how vast a harvest will there be when seeds beyond number have been sown!'" (*4 Ezra* [2 Esdras] 4:26-32 [late first century C.E.])

Jesus tells the parable to the crowds. This fact suggests an expansive quality of storytelling. Matthew's phrase "kingdom of heaven" is a synonym for "kingdom of God." In the parable, a farmer broadcasts good seed in the field. However, an enemy sows darnel in the night. Darnel is a weed. When darnel and wheat sprout, their tiny green shapes are almost indistinguishable. As they grow, they become distinct, but their roots are intertwined. The farmer who tries to pull the darnel will also uproot the wheat. Consequently, the farmer advises the field hands to wait until the harvest to separate them. After the harvest, the darnel is burned to destroy its seeds.

Jesus gives the allegorical interpretation to the disciples. The select audience suggests a quieter, almost secretive, mode of presentation. The allegory applies the parable to Matthew's world: sower of good seed = Son of Man (Jesus); field = world; good seed = children of the rule of God, i.e., the righteous; weeds = children of the evil one; enemy = devil; harvest = consummation of history; reapers = angels; burning of weeds = furnace of fire; wheat in barn = the righteous in the eternal rule of God.

In the context of the first three Gospels, the phrase "son of man" refers to Jesus. It has a special meaning derived from Daniel 7:13-14. It denotes a *heavenly* figure sent by God to act as divine representative in redeeming and judging the world at the time of the apocalypse. According to early Christian tradition Jesus functions as cosmic judge and redeemer.

Jesus and his representatives are doing battle with the devil and the demons in the world. The Greek for "world" is *kosmos*, and in this setting it denotes all that is—humankind and nature. Matthew does not separate the church from the world. The church, as a part of the world, is judged.

Not surprisingly, the world in its present state is ambiguous. Signs and representatives of the rule of God, and signs and representatives of evil, exist side by side. Life in the cosmos is a combat zone. Until the consummation of history, the church can expect wheat and weeds to grow alongside one another. (On the harvest as a symbol of the fulfillment of history, see the earlier discussions of the parables of the sower, Mark 4:1-20, and the seed growing secretly, Mark 4:26-29.)

A complication: the church cannot always distinguish the wheat from the weeds. The community must learn to live through such ambiguity by relying on the knowledge that the day will come when the wheat will be separated from the weeds.

God will send an armada of angels to annihilate evil and to judge all those who have been complicit with it. Matthew uses painful imagery to describe the fate of the wicked. The storyteller might want to speak their destiny in anguish. The angels will throw the wicked into "the blazing furnace, where there will be wailing and grinding of teeth," i.e., into hell. Similar imagery is found in other apocalyptic texts (Daniel 3:6-20; 2 Esdras 7:36). In this world of thought, hell is a means whereby the evil receive the fruits of their disobedience. The fire of judgment is sometimes temporary and for the purpose of refining (Malachi 3:2-4). However, most apocalyptists presume that hellfire is the permanent abode of those who are cast into it.

Who is the darnel in the world? According to 13:41, the angels will gather up "every cause of sin, and all whose deeds are evil." In Greek, the phrase "cause of sin" is *skandala* (from which comes the English "scandal"). This use echoes Zephaniah 1:3, in which the prophet says that God will remove stumbling blocks from the earth. In Matthew, the notion refers to actions that turn away from the divine rule as embodied in Jesus and the church. Both those outside the Christian community (11:6; 13:57; 15:12; 18:7; 24:10) and inside the Christian community can stumble or cause others to stumble (Matthew 5:29-30; 13:21; 16:23; 18:6; 26:31). In Greek, the phrase "deeds are evil" could be translated "people who are lawless" (from the Greek *anomia*, "lawlessness"). For Matthew, the law—especially as interpreted by Jesus—guides the community in the ways of God while it awaits the consummation of history (5:17-20). The lawless disregard the law, particularly by neglecting the practice of justice and mercy. Thereby, they become agents of chaos. The lawless are found both outside (23:28) the church and inside (7:21-23; 24:12).

The angels also gather the righteous, who shine like the sun. This description is similar to that of Jesus during the transfiguration (Matthew 17:2). The image of shining like the sun draws upon Daniel 12:3 and similar uses in apocalyptic literature (*1 Enoch* 39:7; 104:2; 2 Esdras 7:97). After the cataclysm, the saved have bodies but they are transformed (1 Corinthians 15:35-56). They live forever without infirmity or diminishment. They shine like the sun. This eternal existence compensates for the suffering of the present age. By creating the new world, God is proven ultimately trustworthy. Can the storyteller's voice catch the dazzling quality that is prompted by the image of the righteous shining like the sun?

Who is the wheat? The righteous embody right relationships with God and with other people according to the revelation of God in the story of Israel and in Jesus. Righteousness is typically abiding by the law (Matthew 5:17-20). However, as Jesus' indictment of the scribes and the Pharisees shows, following the prescriptions of the law is not in itself a demonstration of righteousness (Matthew 5:17-19; 6:1-6; 6:16-17; 9:10-13; 12:1-8; 15:12-20; 23:1-39). The essence of the law is love, mercy, and compassion (Matthew 7:12; 9:13; 12:7; 20:28; 22:34-40; 23:23). Jesus calls the disciples to the same (5:20). The righteous can be found in Israel (Matthew 1:19; 9:13) and the church (10:40-41), as well as among Gentiles who practice mercy and compassion (Matthew 25:37). However, aspects of this parable leave the listener with several tensions. The church cannot easily identify wheat and darnel. Since God and the angels accomplish the separation, the church is relieved of the anxiety of separating the two. Can the church be patient through the long years when wheat and weeds grow together, relying on God to effect the proper separation at the end of history?

At the same time, the church should not sit by passively and await the judgment. The separation includes the church. The parable pushes the church to consider whether the Christian community is centered in the practice of love, justice, and mercy (that is, fulfilling the essence of the law). Furthermore, the church must sometimes make decisions and take actions that have a judging quality. For instance, the church must sometimes deal with members who disrupt the community (18:15-20). Such members could destroy the community if the church takes no action to redirect their behavior. However, if the church makes a mistake in such matters, it can take solace in the fact that God will rectify all things when the divine rule is fully established. Since God is by nature righteous, all things will be settled rightly. Confidence in divine righteousness provides the church with the means to live through ambiguity.

Retelling the Story

> "'Well then,' they said, 'shall we go and gather the darnel?' 'No,' he answered; 'in gathering it you might pull up the wheat at the same time. Let them both grow together till harvest.'" (Matthew 13:28b-30a)

Once there was a young man who walked into a forest as he walked everywhere, not knowing where he was going. He walked most of the day. It grew dark; the young man looked for a way out of the forest, but he could find none. He spent the night in the forest, cold, hungry, and frightened. He knew that the place was dangerous, but he did not know how to get out.

The next day, the young man began to search again for another way out of the forest. He went down many paths, but no path led him out. He languished in a labyrinth of loss. He was discouraged and then desperate. He spent another night cold, hungry, frightened, knowing that he was going in circles, turning himself around like a top.

On the third day, the young man again searched the many paths to find one that would lead him out of the forest. Still he found none. Suddenly he saw an older man walking toward him. The older man was dressed as if he belonged in the forest.

Rushing to him, the young man shouted, "I'm so glad that I have found you. Thank goodness that you are here. I am lost, and no path I follow leads me out of the forest. Please, help me!"

The older man smiled. "How long have you been lost in the forest?"

"Three days," replied the young man.

"Then why are you so upset? I have been lost for three years."

"Oh no," cried the young man, completely discouraged. "If you have been lost for three years, then it is certain that we will never find our way out. I have searched and searched for the way out. We are doomed."

"No, no—not at all," said the older man. "You see, although I do not know which path leads out of the forest, I know all the paths that do not." *(Corinne Stavish)*

The rabbis also reflected on the difficulty of judging between the good and the evil: "R. Eleazar, son of R. Simeon, once met an officer of the [Roman] Government who had been sent to arrest thieves. 'How can you detect them?' he said. 'Are they not compared to wild beasts, of whom it is written, *Therein [in the darkness] all the beasts of the forest creep forth?*' (Others say he referred him to the verse, *He lieth in wait secretly as a lion in his den.*) 'Maybe,' [he continued,] 'you take the innocent and allow the guilty to escape?' The officer answered, 'What shall I do? It is the King's command.' Said the Rabbi, 'Let me tell you what to do. Go into a tavern at the fourth hour of the day. If you see a man dozing with a cup of wine in his hand, ask what he is. If he is a learned man, [you may assume that] he has risen early to pursue his studies; if he is a day labourer he must have been up early to do his work; if his work is of the kind that is done at night, he might have been rolling thin metal. If he is none of these, he is a thief; arrest him.' The report [of this conversation] was brought to the Court, and the order was given: 'Let the reader of the letter become the messenger.' R. Eleazar, son of R. Simeon, was accordingly sent for, and he proceeded to arrest the thieves. Thereupon R. Joshua, son of Karhah, sent word to him, 'Vinegar, son of wine! How long will you deliver up the people of our God for slaughter!' Back came the reply: 'I weed out thorns from the vineyard.' Whereupon R. Joshua retorted: 'Let the owner of the vineyard himself [God] come and weed out the thorns.'" (*b. Bava Metzi'a* 83b [ca. sixth century C.E.]; from Epstein, 20.477-78)

MATTHEW 13:33 (LUKE 13:20-21)

The Woman and the Yeast

The rule of God is similar to a woman putting a tiny bit of yeast in a massive amount of flour.

The Story

He told them also this parable: 'The kingdom of Heaven is like yeast, which a woman took and mixed with three measures of flour till it was all leavened.'

Comments on the Story

This tiny story has prompted an unusually extensive discussion among scholars regarding its interpretation. I survey two major lines of interpretation and their effects on the storyteller.

Both streams of thought take account of the Matthean context. As noted in our discussion of the parable of the wheat and the darnel, Matthew 13 is a catena, focused on the rule of God, in which each story builds on the preceding one. The parable of the wheat and the darnel pictures the rule of God growing in the world toward a time of harvest and separation (Matthew 13:24-30). The parable of the mustard seed is a story of confidence and contrast. The community is assured of the harvest because God is at work in the world in the same way as a growing mustard seed. While God's presence through the ministry of Jesus and the witness of the church seems as minuscule as a mustard seed, the harvest will be as big as the mustard plant (Matthew 13:32). The parable of the woman and the yeast follows. The rule of God is compared to a woman who leavens a batch of dough.

In a catena, themes continue from one story to the next, but the succeeding story does not simply restate the previous one. The next story adds to the discussion. How does the parable of the woman and the yeast relate to the parable of the mustard seed and amplify the discussion of the rule of God in the catena?

The most widespread interpretation of the story sees the emphasis of the story on the contrast. A woman engages in the first part of an ordinary but important task: preparing bread for baking. She could be a domestic servant or a slave, or she could be a freewoman cooking at home.

Most of the leaven in the ancient world was made by taking a small piece of dough from one day's baking and putting it aside so that it would ferment. This small piece would then be mixed with flour, salt, and water to leaven the next day's baking. Leaven occasionally has positive symbolism in Jewish tradition (for example, Leviticus 7:13-14; 23:17).

The use of the term "mixed" in the Revised English Bible does not catch a subtle Matthean point. Some of the older versions more helpfully translated the word as "hid." The Greek word in this verse *(egkryptō)* is related to a similar word in Matthew 13:35 that is translated "kept secret" *(kryptō)*. Matthew's description of the woman "hiding" the leaven in the lump is an intentional echo of the way in which God has "hidden" the beginning of the divine rule in the ministry of Jesus as well as in the parables.

The woman mixes the leaven into three measures of flour until the whole batch is leavened. Three measures is an extraordinary amount—about fifty pounds, which would make enough bread to feed over a hundred people. The three measures probably allude to Genesis 18:6, in which Sarah prepared three measures of flour for the visitors at the oaks of Mamre. The listener thus associates this large quantity of flour with occasions of revelation.

> Philo, in commenting on Exodus 12:8, understood leaven as a negative image: "(Why) does He say that they shall offer unleavened bread on bitter herbs together with the above-mentioned sacrifice? Unleavened bread is (a sign) of great haste and speed, while the bitter herbs (are a sign) of the life of bitterness and struggle which they endure as slaves. That is the literal meaning. But as for the deeper meaning, this is worth noting, (namely) that that which is leavened and fermented rises, while that which is unleavened is low. Each of these is a symbol of types of soul, one being haughty and swollen with arrogance, the other being unchangeable and prudent, choosing the middle way rather than extremes because of desire and zeal for equality." (Philo, *Questions and Answers on Exodus* 1.15 [first century C.E.], LCL)

The parable, then, contrasts the small amount of leaven hidden in the dough with the huge result. The cosmic consummation of history comes from the tiny beginning of the birth, ministry, death, and resurrection of Jesus.

Another wave of interpretation includes the motif of contrast but takes a different tack on the symbolism evoked by the elements of the story. A woman was low on the social ladder of the ancient world. Hearers are surprised that the reign of God is compared to a woman baking bread.

Yeast has predominately negative associations in the Jewish literature of antiquity. It represents the power of evil, and was to be removed completely from the household at Passover (Exodus 12:15-20). Unleavened bread is used to remember the Passover (Exodus 13:3-10). Yeast was not permitted with some sacrifices (Exodus 23:18; 34:25; Leviticus 2:11; 6:17). Under select conditions, yeast makes the house and sacrifice unclean. Some of the rabbis described the evil inclination in the human heart as yeast.

Negative associations predominate in the Second Testament. Paul warns the Galatians that a little contact with evil (leaven) will spoil the community (Galatians 5:9); that is, the community should avoid the old yeast of malice and evil and celebrate the unleavened bread of sincerity and truth. Likewise Matthew evokes these negative patterns of association. God is like a woman who can take the yeast (evil) of the world and turn it into bread. The rule of God is beginning as Jesus welcomes persons who are unclean (tax collectors, sinners, prostitutes, Gentiles; 9:9-13; 11:19; 21:31).

Also in Matthew the Pharisees and the Sadducees are specifically identified as yeast (16:6). God can transform the evil yeast of the Pharisees and Sadducees into the bread of participation in the rule of God. While the parable does not directly mention bread, the listener naturally extends the process of hiding the yeast in the dough to the raising, kneading, and baking that results in the finished loaf. And, for Matthew (as for several other Jewish writers), an abundance of bread is a symbol of divine providence (as in Exodus 16:4; Wisdom 16:20) and of the presence and bounty of the rule of God (as in Matthew 6:11; 14:13-20; 15:32-39; 26:26; *2 Baruch* 29:8).

Matthew presumes that the people of the world who are yeast, i.e., in alliance with evil, will be transformed through repentance (Matthew 3:2-8; 4:17). Those who do not repent will be condemned.

Luke 9:51 begins the travel narrative (9:51–19:27) when Jesus sets his face to go to Jerusalem and his death and resurrection. Most scholars think that this parable ends the first major section of the Lukan travel narrative (9:51–13:21). Jesus teaches the way of the rule of God (9:51–11:13), encounters opposition (11:14-54), and calls the people to be ready for the consummation of history (12:1–13:21). Jesus warns the disciples to beware of the yeast of the Pharisees, and exhorts them to confess the renewal of the world through Jesus even in the face of opposition (12:1-12). Those who trust in the things of this world will be judged (12:13-21). During the time of suffering, the community does not need to be anxious because God will provide (12:22-34). Instead, they should prepare for the judgment by repenting (12:35–13:9). Jesus then heals the woman who has been bent over for eighteen years (13:10-17) and tells the parable of the mustard seed and the woman and the yeast. The church's confession, repentance, and suffering are part of the yeast that points to the renewal of the world. In addition, as the story in Luke-Acts unfolds, the Jesus movement incorporates people who, like yeast, are unclean (Acts 10–11, 15). Indeed, we learn in Acts 27–28 that the yeast of this movement even includes Rome.

Retelling the Story

"The kingdom of Heaven is like yeast." (Matthew 13:33)

In a time that was and still is, there was an ordinary village with unremarkable people. Things went from worse to worst. The villagers grumbled and cursed, and spoke cruelly to one another. Poverty took up residence instead of visiting frequently. Joy moved to a better place and happiness hibernated. The land mirrored the morale and was brown and wasted.

> Some of the rabbis used leaven (or yeast) as a symbol for the evil impulse in humankind: "According to some this was the prayer of R. Hamnuna, and R. Alexandri on concluding his prayer used to add the following: Sovereign of the Universe, it is known full well to Thee that our will is to perform Thy will, and what prevents us? The yeast in the dough and the subjection to the foreign Powers. May it be Thy will to deliver us from their hand, so that we may return to perform the statutes of Thy will with a perfect heart!" (*b. Berakhot* 17a [ca. sixth century C.E.]; from Epstein, 1.99-100)

The young rabbi decided to take action. He put his knapsack on his back and went to the big city in search of the master rabbi who could give him advice. When he told the master his story, the young rabbi poured out his heart and fears. The master said simply, "I do not know what is wrong with your community. I cannot tell you what to do. But this much I am certain of: One of you is the Messiah."

"What?" exclaimed the young rabbi. "One of us is the Messiah? Are you certain? Who?"

"I do not know," replied the master. "But I am certain it is someone in your village."

All the way back home, the young rabbi contemplated this information. Over and over, he asked himself: "Who? Who could it be? Could it be Shmuel the Shoemaker? What if it is he? No, impossible! Maybe it is Tevye the Tailor? Moshe the Miller? No, impossible! But, what if? And maybe, just maybe, it could be Bayla the Baker?" So the thoughts tumbled in the rabbi's head for miles and miles of walking.

When he got back to the village, everyone surrounded the young rabbi and asked what he had learned from the master. "All I know," said the rabbi, "is that one of us is the Messiah. That is what the master said." The villagers began to run from place to place, shaking with excitement and possibility.

Then they began to think: "Who? Who could it be? Could it be Shmuel the Shoemaker? What if it is he? No, impossible! Maybe it is Tevye the Tailor? Moshe the Miller? No, impossible! But, what if? And maybe, just maybe, it could be Bayla the Baker?"

So, just in case, they each began to speak more civilly to one another . . . just in case. They began to regard one another differently. And then the artificial practice of this behavior became intuitive and sincere, until everyone was treating one another as if he or she might, in fact, be the Messiah. The people began to flourish.

As the people flourished, so did their land. All who visited marveled at the beauty of the town and the well-being of its people. From time to time, one of the villagers still wonders, "Who is it? Which one of us is the Messiah?"

But most now realize that it no longer matters. *(Corinne Stavish)*

The Treasure in the Field and the Pearl of Great Price

The rule of God is like finding a treasure or a valuable pearl and investing one's all in it.

The Stories

The kingdom of Heaven is like treasure which a man found buried in a field. He buried it again, and in joy went and sold everything he had, and bought the field.

'Again, the kingdom of Heaven is like this. A merchant looking out for fine pearls found one of very special value; so he went and sold everything he had and bought it.'

Comments on the Stories

These stories are a pair. While they make a similar point, each does so with its own nuance. Their meaning in Matthew is related to their function in the catena of parables in Matthew 13. (For more on the catena, see my comments at the beginning of the discussion of the wheat and the darnel, Matthew 13:24-30, 36-43.)

Why was the treasure hidden in a field? Palestine was a politically strategic corridor since it connected the various Egyptian empires on the south with other political giants on the north and east. Consequently, other countries frequently invaded Palestine in order to control the travel corridor or to wring tribute out of the local population. So people in the ancient world frequently buried their valuables in order to protect them from the invading marauders as well as from local thieves. A buried treasure could be lost when the landowners were captured (and displaced) or killed.

The treasure itself is not specified. It might have been in the form of coins or valuable objects (such as gold or silver bowls or candlesticks). It could have been placed in the ground in a chest, a clay pot, or even a bag.

The parable does not say how the treasure was found. Most interpreters think that the finder is a day laborer who was ploughing another person's land. Such a worker lived from one day to the next. The blade of the finder's plough might strike the treasure in the soil. The blade might expose the treasure, or the laborer might think it is a rock, and bend over to dig it out. Or the treasure may have worked its way to the surface of the soil and the finder saw it. The laborer was not searching for treasure. The finder was going about a daily routine when, unexpectedly, the treasure appeared.

Should the buyer tell the landowner about the treasure? Should the laborer give the treasure (or part of it) to the landowner? Is the laborer cheating the original landowner? The rabbis and Roman jurists debated such questions. While leading authorities took positions on both sides, the parable assumes that the action is acceptable.

In this rabbinic parallel, the "treasure" is Israel itself: "[It is like] one to whom there fell in inheritance a residence in a seaport city and he sold it for a small sum and the purchaser went and dug through it and found in it treasures of silver and treasures of gold and precious stones and pearls. The seller almost strangled [for rage and grief]. So did Egypt because they sent away [Israel] and did not know what they sent away." (*Mekilta of R. Simon b. Jochai* 14.5 [second century C.E.]; from Boring-Berger-Colpe, 95, no. 103)

First-century listeners would hear an additional connotation. The wisdom tradition often speaks of the awareness of the divine presence and purposes as treasure (Proverbs 2:4; 8:18-21; Isaiah 33:6; Wisdom 7:14). The sages emphasized that the wise act decisively when they have wisdom. Those who find the treasures of God, and respond accordingly, are blessed. Almsgiving, in particular, is such a treasure. Those who practice almsgiving "lay up sound insurance [treasure] against the day of adversity" (Tobit 4:9; see also Ecclesiasticus 29:11). Second Esdras says that those who are faithful to God will be saved from the destruction of the old world; they will be welcomed into the new world because they have laid up a "treasure of faithfulness" (6:5; 7:77). A treasure of immortality awaits the saved (8:54).

Matthew alludes to these associations. In Matthew 6:19-20, Jesus advises the disciples not to store up treasures on earth but to lay up treasure in heaven. Jesus instructs the rich young person who wants to inherit eternal life to sell his possessions, to give to the poor, so that he would have treasure in heaven (Matthew 19:21), i.e., to be included in the reign of God. In its Matthean context, then, to find the treasure and to make the decision to join the rule of God is also to store up treasure in heaven by embracing the reign of God. Matthew mentions almsgiving as a symbol of one's responsiveness to that reign. Almsgiving is also a symbol of God's providential care for all, a care provisionally manifest through the distribution of alms, and ultimately to come about through cosmic renewal.

The finder takes a decisive action and a tremendous risk. As noted, a day laborer lives from day to day. To buy the field, the finder would, literally, be required to sell everything. In so doing, the laborer would leave the household in a precarious position. Further, in the Middle East, land is considered one of the most precious possessions. It is almost unthinkable to part with one's land. In the acts of selling and buying, the day laborer exchanges the proven but limited means of life support for one that is unlimited (by the standards of day labor) but unproven.

The finder is filled with joy. The Matthean listener remembers that the Gentile astrologers who visited Jesus' birth were filled with great joy (Matthew 2:10). The women who discovered the empty tomb were similarly filled with joy (28:8). This joy results from the recognition of the coming cosmic renewal. However, as 13:20 warns, the joy must be disciplined with willingness to endure difficulty, or it will prove ephemeral.

The manifestation of the divine reign is in the world much like the treasure in the field: hidden. Some people can walk over it and not notice. But when they stumble upon it, it can rearrange all priorities if they recognize it for the treasure it is.

The parable of the pearl of great price develops similarly, but with points of difference. In the ancient world, pearls were valuable—in some sectors even more valuable than gold. The sages compare wisdom to fine jewels (Job 28:17-18; Proverbs 3:15; 8:11). Pearls also appear in association with the rule of God (Revelation 21:21). Occasional sayings in Jewish literature use pearls to describe the quality of life in the rule of God. The listener thus hears the transaction on two levels: as a story drawn from the real-life world of commerce, and reverberating with associations with the rule of God.

Whereas the day laborer discovered the treasure accidentally, the merchant is looking for fine pearls. The parable of the pearl of great price thus speaks particularly to those who are searching for the rule of God. This merchant is a major business figure. People of means should feel an affinity with this upper-class character. The parable creates an experience of what they should do when their search leads them to demonstrations of God's ultimate will: take drastic steps to be a part of the rule of God.

Like the finder of the treasure of the field, the pearl merchant takes a risk by selling everything. Indeed, a peculiar complication arises for the pearl dealer. By selling everything in exchange for the one great pearl, the merchant loses the goods and money that enable day-to-day purchases of food and clothing.

In Matthew's narrative context, the parable of the pearl of great price evokes the Matthean teaching about wealth. On the one hand, wealth creates the possibility of witnessing to God's intention to care for all in the world (through almsgiving). Wealth provides for Jesus' burial (27:57). On the other hand, wealth functionally can become an idol (Matthew 6:24). Wealth can choke the desire to say "Yes" to the new world (13:22). Matthew would like hearers of the gospel story to respond to the realm of God in the same way that the Wisdom of Solomon counsels its readers to respond to wisdom. "I valued her [wisdom] above sceptre and throne, and reckoned riches as nothing beside her" (Wisdom 7:8).

The parable of the pearl of great price sets up a contrast with the rich young person in Matthew 19:16-30: "Teacher, what good must I do to gain eternal life?" When Jesus tells him that he must sell all and give alms to the poor, "he went away with a heavy heart," for he was quite wealthy. The hearer is left with this question: As God's rule emerges into its fullness, with whom would I rather identify? The pearl merchant? Or the rich young person?

The manifestation of the divine reign is in the world much like the pearl: waiting to be discovered. Some people search actively for it. When they find it, they take extravagant actions to join it.

Matthew's listeners have responded to the invitation to join the movement toward the completion of God's rule. But Jesus warns them that they may be itinerant (Matthew 8:18-22). They may live with few material goods (10:5-15). Their biological families may disown them (10:34-39; 12:46-50), a particularly heinous development in the Jewish world in the light of the fifth commandment. They will be persecuted (10:16-25). They believe that they are entering into the fateful last days of the old age, the time of tribulation.

Through these parables, Matthew reminds the followers of Jesus that they are wise to seize the pearl of very special value. Indeed, when they sell everything for the treasure hidden in the field, they transfer their treasure from the known world (where valuables are subject to moth, rust, and theft) to the coming world "where neither moth nor rust will destroy, nor thieves break in and steal" (6:19-34). The mention of treasure in 13:44 calls to mind this text, a text that assures the reader of God's ongoing provision for disciples in difficulty even in the great tribulation. Those who sell all that they have for the rule of God discover that the divine realm already supports them day by day. "And anyone who has left houses, or brothers or sisters, or father or mother, or children, or land for the sake of my name will be repaid many times over, and gain eternal life" (Matthew 19:29).

Retelling the Story

> "The kingdom of Heaven is like treasure which a man found buried in a field." (Matthew 13:44)

Once there were three brothers who, after their father died, tended his garden with great love and care. They considered it their inheritance and great treasure. God smiled on their devotion and sent his prophet, Elijah, to visit the brothers with an offer of gifts.

Elijah approached the first brother when he was gardening. "I can offer you one of three gifts. You may have either this jewel that will bring you great wealth, this scroll that will give you great wisdom, or the love of a fine woman."

The first brother took the jewel. Elijah next visited the second brother, who chose the scroll. The third brother wanted the love of a fine woman.

Elijah and the third brother traveled the earth to find this special prize. Elijah consulted with the animals in every town, for he could understand their language and knew that animals saw humans in their true form. When he was satisfied that the third brother had the best woman, Elijah performed the marriage ceremony, wished the couple well, and left.

Many years later, disguised as a beggar, Elijah returned to see how the brothers had used their gifts. He went to the mansion of the first brother, who by now was the wealthiest man in the land, and asked for alms. He received instead blows from the first brother's servant. Elijah then demanded of the brother: "Give me back the jewel I gave you. What good is all your wealth if you cannot share it with one less fortunate?" And even though the brother asked for another chance, Elijah took back the source of the wealth and left the brother in poverty.

The pearl was so valuable in the ancient world that even a monarch would search for one, as related in this rabbinic story: "R. Berekiah b. R. Simon said in R. Nehemiah's name: This may be illustrated by a king who was passing from place to place, when a gem fell from his head. Whereupon the king halted and stationed his retinue there, gathered the sand in piles, and brought sieves. He sifted the first pile but did not find it; the second but did not find it; but in the third he found it. Said they: 'The king has found his pearl.'" (*Genesis Rabbah* 39:10 [fifth century C.E.]; from Freedman, 1.318-19)

He journeyed to the second brother, a wise scholar. Elijah sat in the back of the study house and asked a question. The second brother sneered and said, "You expect someone as wise as I to answer such a simple question?" Elijah demanded the scroll of wisdom back, saying: "What good is all of your wisdom if you cannot answer a simple question?" And even though the brother asked for another chance, Elijah took back the source of the wisdom and left the brother.

He journeyed to the third brother. Before he could approach the small house where the couple lived, the wife ran to greet him and welcomed him into their modest home, in the spirit of Sarah. Elijah stayed the evening, sharing the couple's food, laughter, and stories. Their home was filled with love and joy. And although Elijah knew that the third brother had the jewel and wisdom of his wife, he gave the couple the actual jewel and the scroll to remain in their family, along with their love, for generations to come. *(Corinne Stavish)*

MATTHEW 13:47-50

The Separation of the Great Catch

The rule of God is like a net that catches all kinds of fish so that the good must be separated from the bad.

The Story

Again the kingdom of Heaven is like a net cast into the sea, where it caught fish of every kind. When it was full, it was hauled ashore. Then the men sat down and collected the good fish into baskets and threw the worthless away. That is how it will be at the end of time. The angels will go out, and they will separate the wicked from the good, and throw them into the blazing furnace, where there will be wailing and grinding of teeth.'

Comments on the Story

The story of the separation of the great catch climaxes the catena of parables in Matthew 13. (For more on the catena, see my notes on the wheat and the darnel, Matthew 13:24-30, 36-43.) This parable compares the end of the present age, and the beginning of the new, to the separation of a great catch of fish. The narrative is not an allegory, but its elements prompt resonance in the religious memory of Matthew's listeners. The parable reinforces the earlier themes of the catena, particularly the importance of responding faithfully to the rule of God, by emphasizing the consequences of the great separation.

Such a fishing story was familiar to first-century ears. The net is a seine—a net tied with heavy cord, weighted on the bottom, and equipped with floats along the top. The net is at least six feet deep, and could be as long as a hundred feet. In order to fish, the net is either dropped between two boats and the ends drawn together, or one end is anchored on the shore and the other end carried into the lake by a boat, which then circles the net toward the shore. As the net is drawn, it gathers all kinds of fish. When the net is full, it is pulled onto the shore.

The workers then separated the fish by putting the desirable ones into baskets and by throwing the undesirable ones back into the lake or into a trash pile. The desirable fish are clean and the undesirable are unclean. According to Jewish tradition, fish with fins and scales are clean whereas others are unclean (Leviticus 11:9-12). The clean fish would be scaled and gutted. They would be dried and salted, or pickled, and taken to the marketplace. Some jewelry was made with fish bone. Unclean fish would be thrown away. However, it was unusual to burn them. This end result in the parable may show the fierceness of God's desire to destroy them.

Nets—for use in both land and water—appear figuratively in Jewish literature. Those caught in a net are frequently under judgment (Psalm 66:11; Ezekiel 32:3; Hosea 5:1; 7:12). God's net snares both unfaithful Israel and Israel's enemies. The listener is thus not surprised when the story turns to judgment.

Fish, too, have overtones of symbolic meaning. Fish are sometimes mentioned when Israel is unfaithful, and in scenes of judgment (Nehemiah 13:16; Isaiah 19:8; Ezekiel 29:3-5; 38:20; Hosea 4:3; Zephaniah 1:3; 2 Esdras 16:12; cf. Exodus 7:18-21; Psalm 105:29). When caught, people (similar to fish) are helpless before God (Habakkuk 1:14-17). However, Ezekiel speaks of the waters of the renewed age as filled with many kinds of fish (47:9-10). Because of their division into clean and unclean, fish are a natural symbol for this parable.

> The image of the net catching a variety of fish was used in story form throughout the ancient culture. Here is an example of a Hellenistic story from the "Aesopic" tradition: "A fisherman drew in the net which he had cast a short time before and, as luck would have it, it was full of all kinds of delectable fish. But the little ones fled to the bottom of the net and slipped out through its many meshes, whereas the big ones were caught and lay stretched out in the boat." (*Babrius and Phaedrus* 4 [late second century C.E.]; from Scott, 315)

The listener to Matthew's story will hear an additional undertone in the description of the fish as good (Greek *kalos*) and worthless (*sapros*). When John the Baptist speaks of judgment, he draws on the Jewish use of "fruit" to speak of quality of life to say that the good (*kalos*) tree is the one that bears good fruit and, therefore, is not thrown into the fire (Matthew 3:10). Jesus calls upon his followers to manifest good (*kalos*) works (5:16), i.e., works that illuminate God's realm. Jesus takes up John's image in saying that the good tree bears good fruit (*kalos*) while the poor (*sapros*) tree yields bad fruit (7:17-19). The poor fruit are false prophets who misrepresent God's purposes (7:15-16, 21-23). The good fruit are those who hear the words of Jesus and act on them (7:24-27). People will have to account for the fruit that they bear on the day of judgment (12:33-37). The good (*kalos*) seed matures for gathering in the harvest (Matthew 13:8, 23-24, 27, 37-38). The merchant searches for fine (*kalos*) pearls (13:45). If a hand, foot, or eye causes a person to fall away from faithfulness, that person is better (*kalos*) to remove them than to be "thrown into the fires of hell" (18:8-9).

As the listener hears this parable, the call of the first disciples comes to mind (Matthew 4:18-19). When Jesus called Simon and Andrew to fish for people, he invoked the memory of Jeremiah 16:14-18. In Jeremiah's day, Judah was in collapse. God would send forth many people to fish and catch the people. Some would be caught for the restoration of Israel (16:14-15), but others would be caught so that they might be repaid doubly for their iniquity (16:16-18). The disciples, and the church, are to do the same: cast the net widely and gather as many fish as possible. Indeed, the church itself will be judged on the basis of its casting of the net. But, ultimately, God makes the separation.

The separation of the fish is similar to the judgment of the human family at the end of time. Some commentators contend that Matthew applies this parable only to the judgment of the church. However, when Matthew describes the separation of "the wicked from the good" he uses an expression for "the good" that could also be rendered "the righteous." Furthermore, the phrase "fish of every kind" has a universal ring. The church is a mixed body of the righteous and the unrighteous. But the righteous are also found outside the church (Matthew 25:31-46).

Retelling the Story

> "Then the men sat down and collected the good fish into baskets and threw the worthless away. That is how it will be at the end of time." (Matthew 13:48b-49a)

Once there was a worthy man who prayed to see the World to Come. He wanted to know what his piety would reap for him. Was there a heaven; was there a hell? His prayers were answered. An angel appeared and told him that God was granting his wish to see the World to Come.

They flew east, straight into the rising sun, without feeling any heat. Passing through every time zone, they emerged in a place that had no direction, no color. First they went into a room, an enormous banquet hall. People were seated around tables that were piled high with enormous platters of sumptuous food. The aroma was inviting and invigorating.

"This is Hell," the angel announced.

"Are you sure? Because, if this is hell, what must heaven be like?"

"Look carefully," the angel advised.

Then the man saw what the angel meant. The people were all sitting at the banquet table, which was laden with copious quantities of food, but they were all bone-thin, wasted, and listless, and not one of them was eating. They could not eat. Their hands were all locked into the tabletop, and although they had forks with long prongs that could reach the platters of food, they could not bend their elbows to bring the food from the platter to their mouths.

The visitor watched in horror and echoed what the angel had said: "This IS Hell."

The angel whisked him away to another location. It looked the same: an enormous banquet hall. People were seated around tables that were piled high with enormous platters of sumptuous food. The aroma was inviting and invigorating.

The man noticed that like the people in the other room, their hands were all locked into the tabletop, and although they had forks with long prongs that could reach the platters of food, they could not bend their elbows to bring the food from the platter to their mouths. However, these people were full and robust and smiling.

Then he saw the difference. Although they could not bend their arms to feed themselves, they could eat by feeding one another.

"Ah," he said, "this IS heaven."
(Corinne Stavish)

In a different version of the net parable found in the *Gospel of Thomas* the emphasis is placed on "the wise fisherman" who, in *Thomas,* represents the enlightened person: "And He said to them: 'The man is like a wise fisherman who has cast his net into the sea and drew it up from the sea full of small fish. Among them the wise fisherman found a fine large fish. He threw all the small fish back into the sea and chose the large fish without difficulty. Whoever has ears to hear, let him hear.'" (*Gospel of Thomas* 8 [mid-first to late second century C.E.]; from Scott, 314)

MATTHEW 18:10-14 (LUKE 15:3-7)

The Lost Sheep

Jesus invokes the image of a shepherd who leaves ninety-nine sheep in the wilderness and searches for one lost sheep.

The Story

See that you do not despise one of these little ones; I tell you, they have their angels in heaven, who look continually on the face of my heavenly Father.

'What do you think? Suppose someone has a hundred sheep, and one of them strays, does he not leave the other ninety-nine on the hillside and go in search of the one that strayed? Truly I tell you: if he should find it, he is more delighted over that sheep than over the ninety-nine that did not stray. In the same way, it is not your heavenly Father's will that one of these little ones should be lost.'

Comments on the Story

This is one of the most well known and beloved of the parables. Could we find a Sunday school building that does not have at least one painting of this parable hanging on the wall? Almost without fail, the sheep has a frightened look on its face—its eyes big and white. The shepherd is muscular, and cradles the sheep gently in a crook in the elbow. Such paintings communicate a sense of security as we think of ourselves as lost sheep and God as the great shepherd. However, storytellers need to pay attention to the different ways in which the story appears in Matthew and Luke.

Matthew 18 is the fourth of Jesus' five extended teaching discourses. In this chapter, Jesus instructs the disciples on aspects of living together as a community. Jesus especially provides directions for pastoral care with lost or difficult members. The disciples represent the church. The listener to the Gospel of Matthew thus hears this discourse as instruction to the church.

Jesus begins by comparing the inhabitants of the rule of God to children. This detail is important to the interpretation of the parable. Of course, people in antiquity regarded children as gifts from God who needed proper nurture, but the ancients did not share contemporary North America's sometimes romantic child-centeredness. The dependence and vulnerability of children made them a symbol of those on the margins of life in the ancient world. They are the "little ones" in society. Reversal of current situations is one of the leading themes of apocalyptic literature of the day. In this light, Jesus uses children (representatives of the "least") as symbols of the followers of the rule of God and members of the Christian community. Those who appear least in the old age are witnesses to the new.

Matthew 18:6-7 suggests that some in the community have caused others to fall away from embracing the rule of God. In frightening language ("If your hand or your foot causes your downfall, cut it off"), Jesus advises the disciples to discipline themselves so that they do not fall (18:8-9). The Jewish community did not practice self-mutilation, and so far as we know neither did the early Christians. These words are hyperbole, advising the community to do all in its power to embody the divine rule in community life.

The parable advises the community to seek for members who have fallen away in the same way that the shepherd searches for the lost sheep. Following the parable, Jesus provides the church with instructions on how to go about reclaiming lost sheep (Matthew 18:15-20). Forgiveness plays a prominent role in the search for the lost sheep (18:21-35).

In Matthew 18:10, Jesus tells the disciples not to despise others in the Christian community, for the latter "have their angels in heaven." Many people in the first century believed that God assigned a "guardian angel" to each community. These angels look on the face of God, that is, they receive their instructions from the Holy One; they especially mediate divine providence and judgment. Jesus reminds the church they must answer to God for their treatment of the lost.

The question "What do you think?" activates the listener's imagination. The question directly draws us into the story, and pushes us to come to our own conclusion about it.

A shepherd is in the wilderness with a flock of sheep. The wilderness in Palestine is less like a lush national forest wilderness area in the United States and is more like the semi-arid scrublands of west Texas. Sheep required water and fresh grass. Consequently, the shepherd would keep the flock moving in order to supply the sheep as the sheep would eat a pasture clean and as water and grass supply would change with the seasons. Shepherds followed similar grazing patterns from season to season; along their grazing paths, the shepherds built sheep-pens with rock walls that they used from year to year. The shepherd probably

> The rabbis told a similar parable about counting sheep as a midrash on God's command to Moses to count Israel: "R. Menahema cited R. Bebai's parable of the king who had a flock of sheep which wolves came to rend. Thereupon the king said to the shepherd: Number my flock to find out how many are gone. Even so the Holy One said to Moses: Count Israel to find out how many are gone." (*Pesiqta of Rab Kahana* 2.8 [second century C.E.]; from Scott, 409)

left the ninety-nine in such a pen, and did not leave them standing on the hillside unprotected.

The shepherd seeks to make it possible for sheep to develop optimally. As Psalm 23 suggests, the shepherd guides the flock along safe paths through the wilderness, locates food and water, protects the sheep against danger, and treats their wounds. The shepherd's life is lonely and subject to the elements.

While grazing, sheep often wandered. A sheep could easily catch its foot in a crevice and twist its leg. It might eat a noxious weed that would leave it sick and sluggish. It might cut itself on a briar. When the shepherd called the sheep together, a sheep might well be immobilized.

A hundred sheep is a modest-sized flock. Likely, the owner is the shepherd.

Jewish literature sometimes figuratively refers to the community as a flock and God as a shepherd (Psalm 23; Isaiah 40:11), thus transferring the positive associations of the shepherd and the sheep to the relationship of God and the people. The First Testament also compares the leaders of Israel to shepherds; the leaders of the community are to do in a limited way what God does cosmically: guide the flock. However, at several moments of Israel's history, the community has gone astray (Psalm 119:176; Isaiah 53:6; Zechariah 10:2). Further, Israel's leaders became false shepherds who led the people away from God and toward destruction. Consequently, God will raise up new shepherds, or God will directly shepherd the sheep (Jeremiah 23:1-4; 50:6; Ezekiel 34; Zechariah 10:3-12).

This background extends the question posed at the beginning of the parable. Are the listeners a good flock? And are its shepherds true or false?

Jesus says that the sheep "stray" (Greek *planaō*, "wanderer"; this is the term from which we get our word "planet"). This same Greek term occurs four times in Matthew 24 to refer to those who are misled by false interpretations of the Messiah and of the times (24:4-5), by false prophets (24:11), and by impostors who claim to be messiahs and prophets, who produce great signs and wonders, but who mislead the

> The rabbinic midrash on Psalm 23:1, "The Lord is my shepherd," discusses how God can be compared with such a negative cultural image as that of the shepherd. "R. Jose bar Hanina taught: In the whole world you find no occupation more despised than that of the shepherd, who all his days walks about with his staff and his pouch. Yet David presumed to call the Holy One, blessed be He, a shepherd! But David said: *I understand more from the ancients,* meaning that Jacob called God Shepherd, as it is said *The God who hath been my shepherd all my life long* (Gen. 48:15); so I, too, call God shepherd." (*Midrash on Psalms* 23:1 [ninth century C.E.]; from Braude, *Psalms,* 1.327, via Scott, 414)

church (24:24). Matthew 18 offers a pastoral strategy for dealing with people who stray in these and other ways.

In the parable, a single sheep is so important that the shepherd searches for it. As we hear the story, we feel the sheep's sense of being lost and desolate. And we feel the press of the shepherd's desire to find the lost sheep.

Matthew 18:15-35 prescribes how the community is to search for those who stray. Matthew 18:35 reveals the consequences for straying from Jesus' prescriptions, and for false shepherding.

Matthew 18:14, which is the *nimshal* or application of the story, reminds the auditor that God is the paradigm for the shepherds of the community. The leaders of the church are to search for the lost sheep because God is a seeking and searching shepherd. Indeed, the reference to God's "will" in this verse echoes the prayer that Jesus taught the disciples: "Your will be done, on earth as in heaven" (Matthew 6:10). This motif is consistent with the notion that the disciples are to do in their spheres what God does universally (Matthew 5:48). In so doing, the disciples share in the divine joy. Pastoral searching for the stray sheep is an earthly counterpart of the heavenly will.

In Luke, Jesus uses the parable to reply to the criticism of the Pharisees and scribes that he is eating with tax collectors and sinners. (For the Lukan setting of the story, see our comments on the parable of the lost coin, Luke 15:8-10.) Luke accents the parable a little differently than Matthew. The element of celebration is heightened. We can see the shepherd joyfully lifting the found sheep to the shoulders. We hear the shepherd calling friends and neighbors together to rejoice, and we too feel invited to join the celebration. Jesus then ties being found to repentance (Luke 15:7). In Luke, to repent is to be found. The repentant turn away from complicity with evil and turn toward God. According to Jesus, the tax collectors and sinners fulfill one of the basic requirements for faithfulness: repentance. Therefore, they are welcomed at Jesus' table (Luke 15:2; see also 5:29-32; 19:7).

Retelling the Story

"See that you do not despise one of these little ones." (Matthew 18:10a)

Once there was a man who was pure of heart with a great love for God. He went to the synagogue to pray, but he did not know the words to the prayers. He listened as all the others in the congregation said the words to the prayers perfectly. He knew that he could not worship as they did.

So the illiterate man stood, and with voice raised to heaven, filled with love and devotion, he began to say the alphabet: "Aleph, bet, gimel, dalet. . . . " His voice was so loud that the others stopped praying to listen. When they realized that this ignorant peasant did not know even the simplest prayer, they began to snigger as they looked at one another. Then their quiet giggle turned to laughter and their derision and contempt were open. They rolled their eyes, shook their heads, tittered their disapproval.

When the man finished reciting the alphabet, he began to speak: "Master of the World, you'll forgive me, please. I am an ignorant man, who does not know the simplest prayer. But You, You are Lord of the Universe and know everything. So, please, hear my heart and all the love for You that is in it. I'll recite the letters of the alphabet, to which You gave magnificent shape, with crowns and adornments. You form those letters into the beautiful words for prayers that are acceptable to You. We'll be partners. I'll say the letters; you make the words."

When those who had mocked him heard the man's plea, they grew ashamed and lowered their eyes. Then they heard the peasant weeping as he continued: "Master of the World, Who is Just and Merciful . . . aleph, bet, gimel, dalet. . . . " *(Corinne Stavish)*

The Forgiving Ruler and the Unforgiving Servant

The rule of God is compared to the situation in which a debtor is punished because, though his massive debt is forgiven, he refuses to forgive the small debt of another.

The Story

The kingdom of Heaven, therefore, should be thought of in this way: There was once a king who decided to settle accounts with the men who served him. At the outset there appeared before him a man who owed ten thousand talents. Since he had no means of paying, his master ordered him to be sold, with his wife, his children, and everything he had, to meet the debt. The man fell at his master's feet. "Be patient with me," he implored, "and I will pay you in full"; and the master was so moved with pity that he let the man go and cancelled the debt. But no sooner had the man gone out than he met a fellow-servant who owed him a hundred denarii; he took hold of him, seizing him by the throat, and said, "Pay me what you owe." The man fell at his fellow-servant's feet, and begged him, "Be patient with me, and I will pay you"; but he refused, and had him thrown into jail until he should pay the debt. The other servants were deeply distressed when they saw what had happened, and they went to their master and told him the whole story. Then he sent for the man and said, "You scoundrel! I cancelled the whole of your debt when you appealed to me; ought you not to have shown mercy to your fellow-servant just as I showed mercy to you?" And so angry was the master that he condemned the man to be tortured until he should pay the debt in full. That is how my heavenly Father will deal with you, unless you each forgive your brother from your hearts.'

Comments on the Story

This parable creates a bracing image of the importance of forgiveness in the church. Even more, it assumes that the practice of forgiveness is part of the human response to the rule of God. (On the role of this parable in its Matthean context, see our comments on the parable of the lost sheep, Matthew 18:10-14.)

As the story begins, we encounter a ruler who decides to settle accounts with those who serve him. The story does not indicate the details of the financial arrangements between the ruler and the first servant. The latter might manage the ruler's holdings. Or the servant might be a tax collector who needs to pay the sovereign a share of the taxes collected.

The expression "who owed him" contains a Greek word closely related to the word usually translated "debts," "trespasses," "sins," or "wrong" in the prayer that Jesus taught the disciples in Matthew 6:12. This term recurs throughout the parable. The "debt" or "wrong" can be material in nature (as in this story), or it can be relational. The sensitive interpreter knows that the two are often connected in that a material debt to another often creates a strain in the relationship among those owed and those who owe.

The listener is stunned by the servant's debt: ten thousand talents. The talent was the largest amount of currency in those days. And the number ten thousand was the highest number employed in arithmetic. Herod's annual budget was only nine hundred talents. For purposes of comparison later in the story, ten thousand talents is about fifty million denarii.

When the servant is unable to pay the sum, the sovereign orders his property sold and his family sold into slavery. This action, too, is unusual. The sale of the household would not, of course, cover the amount owed. Ordinarily, the debtor alone would be sold into slavery. The debtor could be put into prison while the family members were left to work out the debt. Indeed, Jewish law at the time of the parable did not allow for the enslavement of family members to pay a debt, although Gentile custom did permit such a move. These anomalies in the story show the freedom of the ancient storyteller to use hyperbole and incongru-

> The rabbis told similar stories of the importance of forgiveness on the human level as compared with the forgiveness of God on the divine level: "Bluria the proselyte put this question to Rabban Gamaliel: It is written in your Law, [she said], *who lifteth not up the countenance,* and it is also written, *The Lord shall lift up his countenance upon thee.* R. Jose the priest joined the conversation and said to her: I will give you a parable which will illustrate the matter. A man lent his neighbor a *maneh* and fixed a time for payment in the presence of the king, while the other swore to pay him by the life of the king. When the time arrived he did not pay him, and he went to excuse himself to the king. The king, however, said to him: The wrong done to me I excuse you, but go and obtain forgiveness from your neighbor. So here: one text speaks of offenses committed by a man against God, the other of offenses committed by a man against his fellow man." (*b. Rosh Hashanah* 17b [first century C.E.]; from Boring-Berger-Colpe, 115-16, no. 140)

ent details to make the story compelling. The ruler's unusual actions show the importance of the debt.

The servant falls at the ruler's feet. This dramatic gesture underscores the depth and desperation of the servant's request. The worker pleads for an opportunity to earn the money. The sovereign is moved with "pity." The Greek term is sometimes translated "compassion" (as in the story of the Compassionate Samaritan, Luke 10:25-37) and refers to feeling empathetically with another.

The ruler gives the servant more than requested. The sovereign forgives the debt. This action creates a new sense of identity for the servant. As one who has been forgiven, he should now be one who forgives.

The servant then leaves the ruler and encounters a second servant. The two are in community as comrade servants; they work together in service to the ruler. However, the second servant owes the first servant one hundred denarii. The first makes a threatening gesture and demands repayment.

A denarius is an ordinary day's wage. For a day laborer, the one hundred denarii is considerable but payable. The contrast between the first debt of fifty million denarii and the second debt of one hundred denarii is dramatic.

The second servant falls at the feet of the first servant and begs for an opportunity to repay the debt. The pathos of the scene is increased when we realize that the second servant's plea to the first servant is spoken in the same words as the first servant's plea to the ruler. The listener remembers Matthew 10:25: "it is enough for the disciple to be like the teacher, and the slave like the master" (NRSV). God's "goodness knows no bounds" (5:48). Instead, the first servant throws the second into jail to pay the debt. While the second servant is in jail, his family will have to work to pay the debt. The first servant's action fractures the relationship between the two servants, and it destroys the social world of the second servant. The parable thus implicitly critiques an economic system that ruptures community.

The community motif continues when other servants, deeply distressed, witness the actions of the first servant and appeal to the ruler. This behavior is reminiscent of Jesus' admonition to the church, earlier in the chapter, to discipline persons who violate community. The listener hears the first servant's action as a violation of the practice for which Jesus taught the disciples to pray (Matthew 6:12). Immediately prior to the parable, Jesus told Peter to forgive other Christians "seventy times seven" (18:22). The number seven represents completeness. Squaring and multiplying by ten are traditional symbols of intensification. Hence, Jesus means, "As many times, and as much effort as it takes." Listeners also recognize the distance between the first servant's behavior and Jesus' instructions in Matthew 5:23-24. Forgiveness between two people takes place when they meet, talk, and come to a resolution.

The final scene of the parable vibrates with intensity. The ruler calls the first servant and reminds him that the massive debt of ten thousand talents had been canceled. The ruler's challenge to the servant is put in the form of a question, a question that the listener to the story is compelled to answer.

The first servant is expected to exhibit his new identity as one who is forgiven by showing comparable mercy toward the second servant. When the first servant fails to do this, the ruler becomes angry and condemns the second servant to be punished, specifically by being tortured.

The reference to torture in this parable could be taken one of two ways. On the one hand, the term originally referred to coin inspection: coins were tested to see that they contained sufficient precious metal to make them worth their face value. This usage was transferred into legal and religious spheres to refer to acts of testing that reveal the truth of a situation, or of a person's assets, heart, or faith (Wisdom 2:19; Ecclesiasticus 4:17; 4 Maccabees 17:10). In some texts, it refers to discipline that is inflicted for the purpose of bringing about repentance (Revelation 11:6-10; cf. 9:20-21; 18:7, 10, 15). In this sense, God hands people over to the consequences of their attitudes and behaviors in the hope that they will come to their senses. On the other hand, torture can refer to situations that are no longer remedial, but are unending (Revelation 20:10; 2 Esdras 13:38). The fate of the first servant exemplifies the truth of Jesus' words in Matthew 7:2 and 12: the servant is treated in the same way that he treated others. Given the prominence of the last judgment in the Gospel of Matthew, the latter option seems to be what is meant. The listener knows, further, that the first servant cannot pay the debt in full while being tortured, nor is the servant's family likely to be able to raise ten thousand talents. Consequently, the prospect of relief is negligible. However, Matthew 18 stresses the importance of reclaiming persons who drift away from the Christian community. The torture could be remedial. The storyteller must decide which angle of interpretation seems most sensible.

The *nimshal* or application of the story then makes explicit the point of the parable. God will consign Christians to torture if they do not practice forgiveness in the community. The importance of forgiveness is again underlined when we realize that the phrase "from your hearts" echoes the commandment to love God (Matthew 22:37).

Some Christians complain that this parable teaches works righteousness. (Works righteousness is the doctrine that one must earn God's love and forgiveness by performing works.) According to this complaint, the first servant must earn forgiveness. However, the parable is clearly predicated upon grace. By canceling the first servant's debt, the ruler does far more than the first servant asks. The first servant does nothing to earn that forgiveness. By accepting the ruler's generosity, however, the first servant accepts a new identity. His problem is that he does not live up to the new identity.

Some Christians do not believe that a God of unconditional love would consign a servant to torture. The storyteller who shares this viewpoint may want to see the story as a vivid image of acts and consequences. Christians who fail to forgive create (and even inflame) ruptures in relationship that can become torturous. God does not put us on the rack; we put ourselves on the rack through our own actions. God continues to hope that our self-caused torment will cause us to repent, and to take actions to restore community.

The parable is clear. The price of not living the life of the forgiven is a kind of torture.

Retelling the Story

> "Then he sent for the man and said, 'You scoundrel! I cancelled the whole of your debt when you appealed to me; ought you not to have shown mercy to your fellow-servant just as I showed mercy to you?'" (Matthew 18:32-33)

Once there was a man of means who was old and ill. He called his only son and said, "My dearest son, I know that I was not the best father when you were growing up, but I had a poor example from my father. He was much too involved in making money when I was a boy. Before he died, he asked for my forgiveness. I, of course, gave it to him. After all, he was my father. However, I made the same mistake and spent too much time with my business and making money and not enough with you. Now, I am old and ill, and, as my father did, I am asking your forgiveness. Unlike my father, I do not want you to wait until I die to have everything that is mine. I can no longer run my business. You and your wife are capable. I will give you my business now. I ask only that you take care of me until I die."

The son merely nodded, not sharing what was in his heart. He and his wife moved into his father's home, taking the finest room for themselves and moving the old man to a small, sparse room. Little by little, they took more and more away from the old man. They sold all of his fine clothes, books, and other possessions and kept the money for themselves. The old man wore rags, and because they were ashamed of him, they made him eat in the kitchen with the servants. Eventually, they moved him out to the barn, where he slept in a corner in his rags. Soon the man and wife forgot the old man was alive.

> This parable reflects an actual practice in the Gentile world. For example, Diogenes Laertius quotes Bion of Borysthenes (third century B.C.E.) who recounted how his father, who was a tax farmer at the time, "cheated the revenue in some way," or, in other words, failed to meet his obligations. He was then "sold [into slavery] with all his family." (Diogenes Laertius, *Lives* 4.46 [third century C.E.]; from Scott, 271 n. 17)

But their son did not forget his grandfather. Each day the child would sneak into the barn and spend time with the old man. The old man embraced the boy, holding him and telling him stories.

Sometimes the boy played alone. The father rarely spent time with his son, but as he was rushing off to work one day, he watched as the child moved rags and blankets from one stack to another.

"What are you doing?" asked the father.

"Well," said the son, "I take some fine blankets from the house and put them in one pile. I take dirty rags and put them in another."

"Why do you play this game?" asked the father.

"Oh, I'm practicing for when I am a man like you. I will have these very fine, warm blankets, and I will save these dirty rags, like the ones grandfather has, for you."

The man realized what he had been doing, and, with tears in his eyes, swept the boy into his arms. Then he went to his father to beg forgiveness for the way he had treated him. The old man forgave him.

Weeping, grandfather, son, and grandson returned to the house. *(Corinne Stavish)*

The Laborers in the Vineyard

The rule of God is like a vineyard owner who hires laborers at different times during the day and, at the end of the day, pays them all as if they had worked the full day.

The Story

The kingdom of Heaven is like this. There was once a landowner who went out early one morning to hire labourers for his vineyard; and after agreeing to pay them the usual day's wage he sent them off to work. Three hours later he went out again and saw some more men standing idle in the market-place. "Go and join the others in the vineyard," he said, "and I will pay you a fair wage"; so off they went. At midday he went out again, and at three in the afternoon, and made the same arrangement as before. An hour before sunset he went out and found another group standing there; so he said to them, "Why are you standing here all day doing nothing?" "Because no one has hired us," they replied; so he told them, "Go and join the others in the vineyard." When evening fell, the owner of the vineyard said to the overseer, "Call the labourers and give them their pay, beginning with those who came last and ending with the first." Those who had started work an hour before sunset came forward, and were paid the full day's wage. When it was the turn of the men who had come first, they expected something extra, but were paid the same as the others. As they took it, they grumbled at their employer: "These latecomers did only one hour's work, yet you have treated them on a level with us, who have sweated the whole day long in the blazing sun!" The owner turned to one of them and said, "My friend, I am not being unfair to you. You agreed on the usual wage for the day, did you not? Take your pay and go home. I choose to give the last man the same as you. Surely I am free to do what I like with my own money? Why be jealous because I am generous?" So the last will be first, and the first last.'

Comments on the Story

The context in Matthew shapes how we hear this parable. The question about divorce (19:3-9) becomes the occasion for Jesus to speak about those who give up their sexual expression for the sake of the rule of God (19:10-12). Jesus then says that the rule of God belongs to those who are like children (19:13-15), i.e., vulnerable, dependent, toward the bottom of the scale of social significance. A rich young person asks Jesus, "What good deed must I do to have eternal life?" Jesus responds that those who are perfect sell all their possessions and give the money to the poor. But the rich young person is unwilling to do so (19:16-22). Jesus cautions the disciples that it is easier for a camel to go through the eye of a needle than for the wealthy to embrace the rule of God. The astonished disciples ask, "Then who can be saved?" Jesus, pointing toward the behavior of the landowner in the parable of the laborers in the vineyard, says, "For men this is impossible; but everything is possible for God" (19:23-26). Unlike the rich young person, the disciples have left much and followed Jesus (4:18-22; 8:21-22; 10:21-23; 10:34-37; 12:46-50). Peter wants to know what reward awaits them. Jesus assures the disciples that in the cosmic consummation of history, their losses will be restored a hundredfold (19:27-29).

"But many who are first will be last, and the last first" (19:30). These words explicitly state the apocalyptic theme of the reversal of fortune between the present and future. Many who appear to be "first" in the present age (the rich young person) will be "last" in the age to come. Many who appear to be last in the present age (the childlike followers of Jesus whose discipleship has caused them to renounce their sexuality, to leave their families, and to give up conventional financial security) will be first in the age to come. As we hear in the parable, God can be trusted to restore a hundredfold all the things that those who witness to the divine rule gave up. But God's faithfulness to longtime witnesses does not cut short divine generosity to those who have only recently joined the witnessing community. The parable illustrates and nuances the saying, "Many who are first will be last, and the last first."

In the parable, Jesus compares the rule of God to the dealings of the owner of a vineyard with five groups of laborers. The parable is not allegorized. Nonetheless, some of the elements of the parable provoke associations from the larger world of Jewish religious

> The rabbis, too, teach the graciousness of God, even toward those who come late to faithfulness. "How do the righteous come [into the world]? Through love, because they uphold the world through their good deeds. How do they depart—also through love. R. Simeon ben Eleazar told a parable. To what may the matter be compared? To a king who hired two workers. The first worked all day and received one denarius. The second worked only one hour and yet he also received a denarius. Which one was more beloved? Not the one who worked one hour and received a denarius! Thus Moses our teacher served Israel one hundred and twenty years and Samuel [served them] only fifty-two. Nevertheless both are equal before the Omnipresent!" (*Semachot Derabbi Chiyah* 3:2 [early third century C.E.]; from Young, 264)

meaning. A vineyard often represents Israel (Isaiah 5:1-7; Jeremiah 12:10; see also our discussion of the parable of the wicked tenants, Mark 12:1-12). The listener recalls that the purpose of the vineyard is to bear fruit for God, that is, to testify to God's purposes for the world. In the Matthean parable, the vineyard appears to represent the line of witnesses to the divine purposes that began in Israel and are now extended into the church.

In the first century, many people who were poor lived in Palestine without regular employment. From one day to the next they worked at different jobs. To secure employment for the day, they would gather before sunrise (about 6:00 a.m.) in the village marketplace, where overseers would come and hire them for the day. A day's pay was a denarius, a subsistence wage that provided basic food and clothing. A landowner would often send an overseer (a permanent employee) to the marketplace to hire laborers. When the landowner personally hires the workers, the listeners are assured of the trustworthiness of the message given to the workers.

The landowner comes again at 9:00 a.m., 12:00 noon, 3:00 p.m., and about 5:00 p.m. Because Palestine had more workers than jobs, unemployed day laborers would often be in the marketplace throughout the day. While not wanting to press the details of the story for too much symbolism, the listener hears the need for increased numbers of workers in light of the coming of the harvest, i.e., the great ingathering of people into the realm of God at the turn of the ages (Matthew 9:37-38; 13:30; 13:39).

The landowner explicitly promises to pay a denarius to the workers hired at sunrise. The landowner tells the workers hired at 9:00 a.m., 12:00 noon, and 3:00 p.m. that they will be paid "whatever is right." The Greek term "right" is in the same word-family as the word "righteous." God, the paradigm of righteousness, does what is right in order to maintain integrity with the divine nature.

At sunset (about 6:00 p.m.), the workday ends. The landowner abides by Jewish law, which provides for day laborers to be paid on the day they work (Leviticus 19:13; Deuteronomy 24:15). When the landowner calls the laborers to be paid, the last hired are paid in the reverse order of their hiring. The workers hired at 5:00 p.m. receive a denarius. When the workers hired earlier in the day see this, they think that they will be paid more than a denarius. They grumble, echoing the murmuring of the Israelites against Moses in the wilderness (Exodus 15:22-24; 16:2; 17:2). Listeners can feel the heat of the day and their tired bodies. Operating with a reciprocal understanding of justice, they want to be paid more than the laborers who came at the end of the day.

The landowner reminds the unhappy laborers that they receive what the landowner promised (20:13). Nothing is denied them. The workers agreed to come to the vineyard for the daily wage. The owner is faithful. Indeed, these workers might have stood all day in the marketplace, unemployed, were it not for the landowner's generosity in selecting them. The listener, of course, remembers the preceding context. Those who are promised a hundredfold in the age to come will receive it. A hundredfold! Now *that* is generous.

The landowner is sovereign. "Am I not allowed to do what I choose with what belongs to me?" The landowner's sovereignty is not exercised capriciously, but is determined by the landowner's character. The listener identifies the landowner with God, especially as revealed in Matthew 5:43-48 when Jesus reminds the listeners that God (the great landowner of the universe) causes the sun to rise on the evil and the good. God's nature is to do more than we deserve. The landowner deals rightly with the workers hired early in the day, while showing unmerited favor to those who came last into the vineyard. According to conventional employment and wage practices, the latter should be impossible. But "everything is possible with God."

The Revised English Bible translates the landowner's last words, "Why be jealous because I am generous?" The sentence in Greek is literally "Or is your eye evil because I am good?" This expression is a first-century metaphor referring to a person whose life is filled with malice, envy, and jealousy toward other people (as in Ecclesiasticus 14:8-10). The workers' grumbling threatens the church's sense of belonging. Indeed, such grumbling may be an example of the kind of sin against the community for which Matthew 18:1-35 provides pastoral guidance (see our discussion of the parables of the lost sheep and the forgiving ruler and the unforgiving servant, Matthew 18:12-14, 23-35).

The vineyard owner's final comment also recalls Matthew 6:22-24. Jewish writers sometimes use the eye as a symbol for perception and understanding. Jesus uses this notion to say that human perception of the world determines our immediate and longtime modes of being. The eye is sound when we perceive (and respond) to God's purposes faithfully (for example, by serving one master, Matthew 6:24). But for those with a bad eye (that is, who try to serve two masters), the world to come will be dark (that is, a place of punishment).

As the parable ends, the landowner is faithful to all the workers. But the landowner's closing remark is a warning to those in the community who are jealous of those who have only recently come into the community. Those who have borne the heat of the day can also feel the heat of hell if they destroy the Christian community by begrudging God's generosity to the laborers who come at 6:00 p.m. This point of view is consistent with Matthew's attitude that the final judgment will also apply to the church (Matthew 7:21-27; 25:31-46).

The landowner's last address to the workers is in the form of a question. This rhetorical strategy has the effect of putting the same question to the listener. Will we put ourselves in eternal danger by begrudging God's generosity to those whom we think unworthy? Will we endanger the Christian community by resenting those who do not measure up to our standards? The storyteller might voice this question so that it lingers in the hearts of the listeners.

Some interpreters hear this story as a near-allegory of the relationship of Jewish people (especially the Christian Jews of Matthew's day) and Gentiles in the rule of God. The workers who came to the vineyard in the early part of the day are said to be similar to persons of Jewish descent, while the eleventh-hour workers are Gentiles who come into the divine rule through the church only in the last hour before the cosmic cataclysm. This telling of the story is compatible with the concern of the early Christian communities to integrate persons from both Jewish and Gentile backgrounds. Before the great landowner of the universe, all are equal.

Retelling the Story

> "When it was the turn of the men who had come first, they expected something extra, but were paid the same as the others." (Matthew 20:10)

Angry is not the word—Joe was *furious*! You could power a locomotive with the steam shooting out from underneath his collar. He kicked a trashcan with his boot and sent it clanking across the worksite, barely missing his coworkers Ted and Billy as they sat in the shade of a shack at the end of a long week's work.

"What'sa matter, Joe?" asked Ted, looking up curiously.

"Just got paid!" Joe shouted.

"You'd think that was good news," said Billy, standing. "We're lucky to even have a job." Times were hard since the stock market crashed and the land dried up. Jobs that paid cash were hard to find in the dust bowl. So when Joe, Ted, and Billy had been hired on to dig irrigation ditches for a local landowner, they had considered themselves to be quite fortunate. The wages were low, but fair, considering the economy. A man could get by on what the landowner paid.

"Good news, heck! We been cheated, boys," Joe said.

"Cheated?" asked Ted and Billy in unison.

"That's right, *cheated*!" Joe said, scowling.

"You mean he didn't pay what he promised?" asked Ted, anger rising up in his chest. "After all our hard work? Lemme see!"

Joe handed Ted a wad of cash. Ted counted it carefully. "Why, it's all here, Joe. Same as last week. I don't see what you're so mad about."

"I'll tell you what I'm mad about," said Joe. "It's him!" He pointed at a young man sitting on the ground by himself and leaning against a truck tire on the other side of the field. The young man's name was Ben. He'd just arrived that morning, walking up in worn-out shoes and asking for a job. The foreman had put him to work alongside Joe, Ted, and Billy.

"Why, what's wrong with Ben?" asked Billy. "He's a good enough worker, ain't he?"

"I reckon he is," said Joe. "But do you figure he's five times better than we are?"

"Five times better?" asked Ted. "What do you mean?"

"That's what he got paid," said Joe. "Five times more than us!"

"What?" said Ted, incredulous. "Five times more!"

"That's what I said," Joe spat. "He got paid a whole week's pay for one day of work. We had to slave all week in this dirt and heat, and he put in just one day, and the boss paid him just as much as us."

"That ain't fair!" said Ted, boiling with rage. "What are going to do about it?"

"Come on!" said Joe. "Let's go talk to the boss!"

The rabbis used a similar image to speak of the goodness and generosity of God. "And so, too, Solomon said to the Holy One, blessed be He: Master of the universe! When a king hires diligent workmen, and they do their work well, and he gives them their pay, should the king be praised? When is he to be praised? When he hires slothful workers, but gives them their pay in full." (*Midrash on Psalms* 26:3 [ca. ninth century C.E.]; from Braude, *Psalms*, 1:359)

The three of them stomped across the gravel and approached the foreman, who stood talking with Mr. Fairchild, the landowner.

"Excuse, me, sir," said Joe to the foreman. "We'd like to have a word with you."

"Alright," said the foreman. "What's on your mind?"

"It's just that . . . it ain't fair, what you paid us," Joe said.

"Is that right?" said the foreman. "Perhaps you'd like to speak with Mr. Fairchild here. He's the one that hired you."

Mr. Fairchild, the landowner, spoke to Joe gently. "Is there a problem with your pay, Joe? Didn't I pay what I promised? Or do you think my wages are not fair?"

"No, sir. Your wages are fair enough. We got paid exactly what you promised. It's just that, you see, the problem is, it's not fair that you paid that new worker, Ben, five times more than us. I mean, we worked hard all week and he worked just one day, and he got paid same as us. I just figure that we're worth a whole lot more than him. I mean, begging your pardon, but he's new on the job, and we've been with you a lot longer. It just ain't fair. You ought to pay us a lot more than him."

Mr. Fairchild put his arm around Joe's shoulder. "You're a good man, Joe. You're a good worker, and I pay you an honest dollar for an honest day's work. Please don't be angry with me for being generous with Ben. I have my reasons. I know him, and I know his family. Believe me, he could use a little help right now."

Joe thought about it for a moment. Then he looked back at Ben again and saw him in a new light. By golly, he *did* look like he could use a little help right now.

"Oh, alright," he said. "By the way, do you need us next week?"

"I sure do," said Mr. Fairchild. "I'll see all of you Monday morning."

"See you Monday," said Joe. *(Randy Graves)*

Two Children in the Vineyard

Responses to Jesus are compared to the differing responses of two siblings who are asked by their father to work in the vineyard.

The Story

But what do you think about this? There was a man who had two sons. He went to the first, and said, "My son, go and work today in the vineyard." "I will, sir," the boy replied; but he did not go. The father came to the second and said the same. "I will not," he replied; but afterwards he changed his mind and went. Which of the two did what his father wanted?' 'The second,' they [the chief priests and elders] replied. Then Jesus said, 'Truly I tell you: tax-collectors and prostitutes are entering the kingdom of God ahead of you. For when John came to show you the right way to live, you did not believe him, but the tax-collectors and prostitutes did; and even when you had seen that, you did not change your minds and believe him.'

Comments on the Story

The context in Matthew provides important interpretive perspectives on this parable. Jesus enters Jerusalem (21:1-11). In a prophetic gesture that prefigures the destruction of the temple, he overturns the tables of the moneychangers (21:12-13). Jesus enters into conflict with the chief priests—the leaders of the temple—and the scribes (21:14-17) and causes the fig tree to wither, an act that also symbolizes the destruction of the temple (21:18-22). The chief priests and elders challenge Jesus' authority. When Jesus seizes the initiative and challenges them, their reply reveals their spiritual bankruptcy (Matthew 21:23-27). The scene is ironic: the one who is questioned turns around to question the questioners. The setting contributes to Matthew's negative presentation of the temple leadership, the scribes, and the elders.

The parable begins with a question. The question asks the auditor to think about the story that follows and to respond. The storyteller might speak the question so as to direct the "you" to the contemporary congregation. A pause after the question would let it soak into the minds and hearts of the listeners.

The presence of the vineyard calls forth much the same reaction from auditors as in the parable of the laborers in the vineyard (Matthew 20:1-16) and the parable of the wicked tenants (Mark 12:1-12), discussed previously. The vineyard is to bear fruit. In Jewish thought, fruit is a metaphor for manifesting God's purposes in thought, feeling, and action.

The parent is a vineyard owner or manager. The parent asks the first child to work in the vineyard. The expression "my son" communicates endearment and affection. The parent asks the child to go to the vineyard *today*. The reference to "today" gives the request an urgent quality. This child agreed to do so, but did not.

The parent goes to the second child with the same request. This child initially refuses the invitation, but then has a change of mind and works in the vineyard. The Greek word for "has a change of mind" is not the usual early Christian word for "repent." However, the use of the latter in 21:32 suggests that the second child's "change of mind" was an act of repentance. The story does not indicate what caused the change of mind.

Jesus then asks which of the two did what the parent wanted. The storyteller could set off this question with pauses so that contemporary listeners are invited to respond to it. When the chief priests and elders answer the question correctly, they condemn themselves (after the manner of David condemning himself in the wake of Nathan's story about the owner of the ewe lamb in 2 Samuel 12).

> The rabbis emphasize that even if one has abrogated one's promises to God, God welcomes the repentant. "R. Samuel Pargrita said in the name of R. Meir: This can be compared to the son of a king who took to evil ways. The king sent a tutor to him who appealed to him saying, 'Repent, my son.' The son, however, sent him back to his father [with the message], 'How can I have the effrontery to return? I am ashamed to come before you.' Thereupon his father sent back word, 'My son, is a son ever ashamed to return to his father? And is it not to your father that you will be returning?' Similarly, the Holy One, blessed be He, sent Jeremiah to Israel when they sinned, and said to him: 'Go, say to my children, "Return."'" (*Midrash R. Deuteronomy* 2:24 [ca. second century C.E.]; from Freedman, 7.53)

The words "did what the father wanted" could be translated "who did the will of his father." The expression sparks the memory of the third petition in the prayer that Jesus taught the disciples: "your will be done, on earth as in heaven" (Matthew 6:10; cf. 7:21; 12:50; 18:14). God's will is God's rule. That rule is already fully exemplified in heaven. The workers in the vineyard are to demonstrate its character and purposes on earth.

From my point of view, neither child makes an *optimum* response to the parent's request. The first is hypocritical—saying one thing, and doing another. The second initially shows a lack of respect for the parent. Indeed, in the ancient Near East, disregard for the parent was a serious violation of family relationship. Of course, the second child eventually has a change of mind. But the second sibling could have contributed much more to the vineyard by making an immediate, initial, positive commitment.

Jesus then applies the parable to the chief priests and elders. By saying "Truly I tell you," Jesus uses a solemn expression that frequently introduces sayings about the judgment of the last days.

Tax collectors were despised because of their collusion with Rome (see further the parable of the Pharisee and the tax collector, Luke 18:9-14). Prostitutes were reviled because they distorted the purposes of sexuality. In the world of the Bible, sexuality was considered a divine gift for the purposes of procreation, for embodying the intimacy of knowledge and the bond between spouses, and for its pure passion in the context of love (Song of Songs). Some religions of antiquity taught that human beings achieve unity with a deity through sexual intercourse with a sacred prostitute, a person appointed by the cult to mediate the divine presence through sexual expression. Israel particularly loathed sacred prostitutes because they served idols. According to Ecclesiasticus 26:22, a prostitute is regarded as spittle.

The expression "entering the kingdom of God ahead of you" means that the chief priests and elders are denied a place in the rule of God. That sense is consistent with John's verdict in Matthew 3:10-12 and with the two parables that follow (21:33-43; 22:1-14).

Why are tax collectors and prostitutes embraced in the rule of God when the chief priests and elders are not? The chief priests and elders did not act on the instructions of John the Baptist when he told them "the right way to live," i.e., "the way of righteousness." Righteousness is doing what is right according to God's intention. According to John, repentance is the first step on the path of righteousness (Matthew 3:7-9). To repent is to turn away from the old age and its destructive phenomena and rulers (idolatry, injustice, violence, the demons, Satan) and to turn toward God and the new world with its abundance, justice, and peace. Judgment and destruction are the consequence of failing to repent (Matthew 3:10-12). The chief priests and elders did not believe John. They bore bad fruit. By the time of the Gospel of Matthew, the listener knows that the temple—the center of power for the chief priests—has been destroyed, and with it the need for a priestly group. So to the community of Matthew, John's words have come true: God has laid the axe to the root of the temple.

In contrast, the tax collectors and prostitutes repent. They are regular participants in the rule of God as it is unfolding through the ministry of Jesus (Matthew 9:9-11; 10:3; 11:19). They are blessed because they "hunger and thirst to see right prevail" (Matthew 5:6).

The parable warns those of Matthew's day that a fate similar to that of the chief priests and elders awaits those who say "Yes" to God's invitation to work in the vineyard but then fail to do so. These persons include Christians in Matthew's world. "Not everyone who says to me, 'Lord, Lord' will enter the kingdom of Heaven, but only those who do the will of my heavenly Father" (Matthew 7:21). On the positive side, blessing awaits those who respond positively to Jesus' invitation.

Retelling the Story

"Which of the two did what his father wanted?" (Matthew 21:31a)

It was a bumpy ride to the sale barn. With every rut in the road my head rolled from side to side and my elbows jostled my dad on my left and my older brother Tim on my right as we sat in the cab of the old Ford. I felt sorry for the load of heifers we were hauling in the trailer behind us, poor dumb animals on their way to market. Truth be told, though, I'd have rather been back there with the cattle than sitting between my dad and brother that day.

Dad was grinding his teeth, he was so mad. His hands were gripping the wheel like a man handles a hoe to kill a snake, and I could tell that he was really working up a good chewing-out. My brother Tim sat sullenly with his arms crossed and the brim of his cap pulled low as he stared out the window. He was mad at me and Dad, Dad was mad at him and me, and I was mad at both of them. So much for pleasant conversation. There wasn't any conversation at all. It was the meanest kind of angry, the silent kind.

But then Dad took a curve a little too fast and I slid across the seat and collided with Tim. "Will you quit bumping me!" he snapped.

"I can't help it," I protested. "This darn road is washed out." I knew better than to criticize my dad's driving.

"Just stay away from me," Tim said. And then, out of pure meanness, he elbowed me a good one in the shoulder.

"Ouch!" I said. "What are you so mad about, anyway? Besides, it's your fault we're so late. If we miss the sale, you're to blame, not me!"

Well that did it. Tim shouted at me, "How is it *my* fault? I can't help it the four-wheeler quit!"

"You could have saddled up, same as me, but no, you just had to tinker with that engine all morning long while I'm out there trying to cull 'em on my own."

Tim glared at me. "You were not. You rode down to the creek, just like you always do when you're mad. Lord knows what you do down there."

"I had to clear my head," I said. "I came back. Besides, I'm sick and tired of being the only one to pull my share. You're always finding excuses not to work."

What happened was, Dad had to go up to Goshen to help Mr. Bailey pull a calf, and so he told Tim and me to cull the heifers for market. It's a three-man job, but two can do it if they have to. Tim said he'd do it, but then he got sidetracked like he always does. When I saw him tinkering with that four-wheeler, I knew I'd end up doing all the work myself. As Dad was heading out the door, he told me to get on out there and get to work, and I just sort of snapped. I'd had enough. "I don't feel like it!" I said. But then I went out to the barn anyway and saddled up. Tim was still tinkering away.

> For the rabbis, saying "Yes" to God invokes the responsibility to do what God asks and says. "R. Simeon b. Halafta said: If one learns the words of the Torah and does not fulfil them, his punishment is more severe than that of him who has not learnt at all. It is like the case of a king who had a garden which he let out to two tenants, one of whom planted trees and cut them down, while the other neither planted any [trees] nor cut any down. With whom is the king angry? Surely with him who planted [trees] and cut them down. . . . Whence this? For it is said, *Let favour be shown to the wicked; he has not learnt righteousness* (Isa. XXVI, 10). But if he has learnt and has not fulfilled, no favour will be shown to him. Hence the force of, *To observe to do all His commandments.*" (*Midrash R. Deuteronomy* 7:4 [ca. second century C.E.]; from Freedman, 7.135)

I said to him, "Just take Ma Kettle," referring to our old swayback mare.

"I can't ride her," he said. "I'll have this four-wheeler fixed shortly. You go on out and I'll join you in a bit."

I'd heard that before. Tim loves to tinker with engines, and he can waste more time fixing things than it would take to do the job without them. I got so mad, I rode out to the creek to clear my head. I wasn't gone more than an hour or so before I went back and began culling out the heavier heifers on my own. By the time Tim came out with the four-wheeler to help, most of the morning was gone and we saw Dad's truck coming up the road. That's when we realized that we were in a load of trouble.

With the three of us working, we managed to get 'em culled and loaded into the trailer, but we were running so late, the sale barn was likely to be closing up by the time we got there. Even if there were some buyers left, we weren't likely to get a good price. Dad had a bank note due and property taxes and who knows what all. We weren't ruined, but we were sure set back a bit, especially if we had to wait another week to market the heifers. Now everyone was mad at everyone else. Tim was blaming me, and I was blaming him. Now I ask you—who do you think was to blame?

I thought Dad was going to blow up listening to us. But he remained silent, and I've never seen him so mad before. But then, as we drove up to the sale barn and saw that there were just a few trucks left, he let out a long sigh.

"I'm disappointed in both of you," he said quietly, not looking at us. He sighed again, and it had the sad sound of a tire going flat. As he got out and walked up to the barn, Tim and I sat silently, looking at each other in the truck and listening to the cattle low. *(Randy Graves)*

The Wedding Banquet

The rule of God is compared to a wedding banquet that the first invited refuse to attend but that the last invited gladly attend.

The Story

Jesus spoke to them again in parables: 'The kingdom of Heaven is like this. There was a king who arranged a banquet for his son's wedding; but when he sent his servants to summon the guests he had invited, they refused to come. Then he sent other servants, telling them to say to the guests, "Look! I have prepared this banquet for you. My bullocks and fatted beasts have been slaughtered, and everything is ready. Come to the wedding." But they took no notice; one went off to his farm, another to his business, and the others seized the servants, attacked them brutally, and killed them. The king was furious; he sent troops to put those murderers to death and set their town on fire. Then he said to his servants, "The wedding banquet is ready; but the guests I invited did not deserve the honour. Go out therefore to the main thoroughfares, and invite everyone you can find to the wedding." The servants went out into the streets, and collected everyone they could find, good and bad alike. So the hall was packed with guests.

'When the king came in to watch them feasting, he observed a man who was not dressed for a wedding. "My friend," said the king, "how do you come to be here without wedding clothes?" But he had nothing to say. The king then said to his attendants, "Bind him hand and foot; fling him out into the dark, the place of wailing and grinding of teeth." For many are invited, but few are chosen.'

Comments on the Story

Our remarks above about the context of the parable of the two children in the vineyard (Matthew 21:28-32) also apply to the parable of the wedding banquet. For the latter is the third in a series of stories in succession with related purposes. At one level, these stories critique some Jewish leaders for failing to respond adequately to the fresh manifestation of God's rule through Jesus. At another level, Matthew uses the fates of the characters in the stories to warn the Christian community not to be complacent in their witness. Christians, too, will be judged, and they can be condemned.

The parable compares the coming of the rule of God to the events that transpire as a ruler arranges a banquet for his child's wedding. Jewish and early

Christian literature represents the consummation of history as a wedding and as a banquet (Isaiah 25:6-8; 62:1-5; *2 Baruch* 29:4-8; *1 Enoch* 62:14; Mark 2:19; Revelation 19:1-6; 21:1-9). While the parable is not a fully developed allegory, the mention of the "son" prompts the listener to think of this character as a symbol for Jesus. First-century wedding customs, with their extended celebration involving the whole village, were evocative representations of the coming of God's reign (see further our discussion of the parable of the ten young women awaiting the bridegroom, Matthew 25:1-13).

Another dimension of the invitation is more subtle. Matthew draws on the wisdom tradition to help interpret Jesus. For instance, Jesus' invitation in Matthew 11:28-29, "Come to me, all who are weary . . . ," is similar to Wisdom's invitation in Ecclesiasticus 51:26-27. Jesus is embodied wisdom. In Proverbs 9:1-18, Wisdom, personified as a woman, sends servant girls to invite the listeners to her banquet, at which they will learn to distinguish the ways of God (9:1-12) from the foolish woman whose food leads to destruction (9:13-18). Matthew's mention of the bullocks and fatted beasts is similar to the description of wisdom's meal (9:2). The listeners thus understand that they must make a choice.

In antiquity, it was customary to invite guests to a banquet in two phases. The banquet-giver first sends messengers to the guests, several days in advance, to invite them and to tell them to be ready at an approximate time. The second invitation is sent when the feast

The rabbis used a similar image of proper dress at the great banquet in the afterlife to refer to Torah observance. "[A king invited guests to a banquet.] He said to them, 'Go, wash yourselves, brush up your clothes, anoint yourselves with oil, wash your garments, and prepare yourselves for the banquet,' but he fixed no time when they were to come to it. The wise among them walked about by the entrance of the king's palace, saying, 'Does the king's palace lack anything?' The foolish among them paid no regard or attention to the king's command. They said, 'We will in due course notice when the king's banquet is to take place, because can there be a banquet without labor [to prepare it] and company?' So the plasterer went to his plaster, the potter to his clay, the smith to his charcoal, the washer to his laundry. Suddenly the king ordered, 'Let them all come to the banquet.' They hurried the guests, so that some came in their splendid attire and others came in their dirty garments. The king was pleased with the wise ones who had obeyed his command, and also because they had shown honor to the king's palace. He was angry with the fools who had neglected his command and disgraced his palace. The king said, 'Let those who have prepared themselves for the banquet come and eat of the king's meal, but those who have not prepared themselves shall not partake of it.' You might suppose that the latter were simply to depart; but the king continued, 'No, [they are not to depart]; but the former shall recline and eat and drink, while these shall remain standing, be punished, and look on and be grieved.' Similarly in the Hereafter, as Isaiah declares, *Behold, My servants shall eat, but ye shall be hungry* (Isa. LXV, 13)." (*Midrash R. Ecclesiastes* 9:8 [eighth century C.E.]; from Boring-Berger-Colpe, 125-26, no. 159)

is prepared; the guests are now to come. Evidently, the ruler in the parable had sent the first invitation prior to the action in 22:3-4. Matthew 22:3 is the second invitation. However, to the listener's dismay, the first set of guests violates ancient mores of hospitality by refusing to come. Indeed, the refusal of a monarch's invitation was tantamount to rebellion (2 Samuel 10:4). Listeners are surprised by the sovereign's unusual action of making third (22:4-6) and fourth invitations (22:8-10). The extra invitations demonstrate the strength of the ruler's desire to have a complete wedding celebration, replete with a full complement of guests.

In the same manner as the previous parable of the wicked tenants (Matthew 21:33-43), the series of invitations and responses corresponds to the history of Israel and the church. God has continuously sent servants to invite Israel and the church to join the wedding banquet. The prophets are sometimes described as "servants" (Jeremiah 25:4; Amos 3:7; Daniel 9:6; Revelation 10:7; 11:18). Matthew identifies some early Christians as prophets (5:17; 7:15; 10:41; 23:34; 24:11, 24).

The first group to receive the invitation, having no reason to refuse, is rude. The parable's description of the second invitation is fuller and more sensual. We can see and taste the bullocks and fatted animals. Two of the invitees, the farmer and the businessperson, turn their backs on the invitation and return to their business affairs. However, the king expected them to have their affairs in order so that they can come when the announcement of the banquet arrives. Still others seize the servants, attack them brutally, and kill them. The latter image invokes the notion that Israel rejected the prophets (Matthew 23:31-39) and persecuted Jesus and early Christian witnesses (Matthew 10:16-26; 24:9-24).

The ruler is furious. The sovereign sends a military force to destroy the murderers and burn their town. First-century auditors recognize the destruction of Jerusalem in this part of the story. Matthew draws on imagery from Isaiah 5:24-25 to offer the reader a theological interpretation of the sack of Jerusalem: when the leaders of Judaism turned away from Jesus and the manifestation of the divine rule, God condemned the city.

The wedding banquet, however, is still ready. So the monarch sends the servants into the streets to invite everyone they can find. The expression "into the streets" refers to the point on the edge of the city where the streets pass through the walls and become country roads. Whereas the ruler was acquainted with the inhabitants of the town from which the first groups of guests were invited, the ruler does not know these people who live in the countryside. The language of Matthew 22:10 reminds the reader of Jesus' commission to the disciples to go "to all nations" (Matthew 28:19-20).

The wedding hall is packed. However, admission does not guarantee a place at God's banquet table in the age to come. For the servants invited "good and bad alike." As we have noticed several times, the present church is a mixed community whose members will be separated for eternal life and eternal punishment at the great judgment (Matthew 7:13-28; 13:36-43; 13:47-50).

The theme of the judgment of the church is reinforced by Matthew 22:11-14. In those days, people wore special festive garments to weddings. The monarch questions why a guest has come to the wedding in street clothes. The reader should hear this exchange from the point of view of Jewish tradition in which freshly washed garments represent a life that manifests God's purposes (Isaiah 61:10; Zechariah 3:3-5; Revelation 3:4, 5, 18; 19:8; 22:14; *1 Enoch* 62:15-16). Some early Christians also speak in the language of dress to describe the transition from the old age to the new. Paul, for instance, speaks of "putting on" Christ to represent this transition (Romans 13:14; Galatians 3:27; Ephesians 4:24). The listener understands these garments to include the "fruits" of faithful obedience through proper thought, feeling, and action that Matthew so often stresses (Matthew 3:8-10; 7:17-19; 12:33; 13:23).

When the guest has nothing to say, the ruler condemns the ill-dressed person to be bound hand and foot and flung into the darkness, "the place of wailing and grinding of teeth." The binding of the hands and feet tells the listener that the verdict is severe. The dark place of wailing and grinding of teeth is an emotionally chilling and oft-repeated image for the realm of eternal punishment (Matthew 13:42, 50; 24:51; 25:30). Perhaps the storyteller could speak this part of the story so that the listeners feel the pain of those in the darkness.

The final saying is a solemn summary of the point of the parable. God has invited a lot of people, over several centuries, to partake of the divine banquet. However, only a few have chosen to do so. As the parable makes clear, the few are not chosen on the basis of divine arbitrariness. In a sense, they choose themselves by responding fully to God's invitation to join the new world represented by the banquet.

The intent of this parable is to encourage listeners to live so that they can be a part of the divine banquet that is already beginning in the world. However, the story attempts to motivate the community through its sobering, even frightening, conclusion. The preacher or teacher might honor the intent of the parable and yet shift the presentation of the story to a positive axis. What might lure today's people to want to respond positively to God's invitation to the wedding banquet? Of course, rejecting God's invitation does have negative consequences. If we accept God's invitation, but do nothing to act upon it, we deny ourselves the joy of feasting at God's table.

Luke's version of the story explains that participation in the rule of God (including its prefiguration in the church) is dependent upon responding affirmatively to God's invitation. The conventionally secure (the landowner, the oxen-buyer, the person just married) reject the invitation and exclude themselves from the banquet hall. When the poor, crippled, blind, and lame (traditional representatives of the vulnerable in Jewish literature) do not fill the banquet hall, people are welcomed from the roads and the lanes. The last probably represent Gentiles.

The listener in the first century would recognize a situation in which the three refusals, similar to the ones in the parable, are socially acceptable: holy war. Participation in a holy war was considered one of an Israelite's most important obligations. Deuteronomy 20:5-7 lists three reasons for not serving in holy war: building a house and yet not living in it, planting a vineyard without tasting its fruit, and marrying without performing the sexual consummation. Indeed, according to Deuteronomy 24:5, the newly married are released from a number of social obligations for a year. However, the parable emphasizes that this invitation takes precedence even over holy war and its regulations, for it is an invitation to the rule of God as manifest through Jesus and the church. God's invitation makes its claim over even the most important life commitments.

The parable in Luke assures the poor, the crippled, the blind, and the lame (and those whom they represent) that they are welcome at God's table in the community that anticipates the new age. The parable also reminds the community that it is actively to offer regenerative ministry to those who are as vulnerable in any age as the poor, the crippled, the blind, and the lame in the world of Luke. The Christian community that is made up only of landowners, oxen-owners, and the happily married is only a partial reflection of God's concern. The Lukan parable further invites those of conventional religious viewpoint and economic means to take the appropriate steps to allow them to join the poor, the crippled, the blind, and lame in the church and in the age to come. They, too, can taste God's banquet.

Retelling the Story

> "The wedding banquet is ready; but the guests I invited did not deserve the honour. Go out therefore to the main thoroughfares, and invite everyone you can find to the wedding." (Matthew 22:8-9)

You didn't have to see them a-comin' to know they was there. You could smell 'em a mile away. They were the Chicken Ketchers. They lived in hidden shacks way out in the sticks, three or four families to a shack, on property owned by the Acme Chicken Corporation. They worked six, sometimes seven days a week, up to twelve hours a day. My job was to transport the men piled into the bed of a dump truck from chicken coop to chicken coop in the suffocating heat. Their job was to catch the chickens, plain and simple. When they entered the coops, it sounded like the gates of hell had been flung wide open, to hear the screams and squawks of those chickens as they beat their wings and scratched and pecked the hands and faces of the men trying to catch them. And the smell? Phew! It was gawdawful! The coops were nauseatingly nasty. As the Chicken Ketchers scrambled after the terrified chickens, it fairly rained chicken filth down on their heads. By the time they were finished with the long day's work, the Chicken Ketchers were fairly covered with filth from the tops of their heads to the soles of their shoes. They were beaten and bruised and all scratched up, and they smelled awful. It was a rough life for the Chicken Ketchers.

I never knew why they'd take such a menial job. I mean, nobody from around here would do it, I don't care how hungry they were. But then one day I started talking to one of the Chicken Ketchers. His name was César. He was a little man, always quiet and soft-spoken, but he spoke American pretty good, and so I struck up a conversation with him. We were at the annual company barbeque, and I noticed him standing in line right beside me. I didn't recognize him at first. Normally whenever I saw him, he was covered in filth. But today he was cleaned up right nice in his white dress shirt and khaki pants, and he had a nice smile. To tell you the truth, I was surprised to see him there, because the illegals were supposed to stay hidden, but the company president himself had invited them, so I guessed it was okay.

"How ya doing, Pedro?" I asked him.

"César," he said. "My name is César." He shook my hand firmly with a grip accustomed to grabbing chickens. So we began chatting, and eventually I got around to asking him why he wanted to be a Chicken Ketcher. He looked at me kind of odd, and told me his story.

César was from a small Mexican town across the border, not far from Brownsville, Texas. Apparently, they have it pretty bad over there: no money, no food, no jobs, no running water or electricity. His children were going hungry, so César did what any man would do—he took whatever job he could get. One day a man showed up from the Acme Corporation and offered him and his brothers all good jobs at a chicken plant in Arkansas. It was all "off the record," so they didn't have to worry about getting no green cards.

One night at midnight the Acme Corporation sent three trucks with live chickens all piled into little cages stacked on top of each other. They'd made a little tunnel where the illegals could squeeze through the cages and pile into a hollowed out place in the middle of the truck bed, and then they were sealed in with crates of chickens piled behind to hide them. They rode that way, surrounded by the cages and getting dripped on by the chickens, for sixteen hours. Eventually, they were dumped on company land to live in the cramped little shacks and work the coops. Every two weeks, they sent most of their meager pay back home to feed their families.

César smiled as he told me his sad story. It was as if he was afraid to tell me the truth about how much he hated being a Chicken Ketcher. I can't say that I blame him. We went through the line and filled our plates with corn on the cob, baked beans, potato salad, and cole slaw. He passed by the meat.

"What's wrong?" I asked. "Not hungry?"

"I don't eat chicken," he said, laughing.

I sat at the picnic table with him and his brothers. I couldn't understand a word they said, but from time to time César would talk to me or tell me a joke one of them had said. They seemed happy to be sitting together in the sun, enjoying the food and the laughter.

Halfway through the dinner, I realized why the president had invited them. They were the entertainment. The president called them to the stage, and César and his brothers all picked up guitars of various sizes and began to play the yearning songs of Old Mexico. I couldn't understand the words, but their voices took me to another place and another time. Their songs made me think of towering palaces, of soaring eagles, of grand sweeping rivers and plateaus full of grain, and of noble human princes echoing strains of the Divine. *(Randy Graves)*

MATTHEW 24:45-51 (LUKE 12:41-48)

The Faithful and Unfaithful Servants

A lesson is drawn from a story about servants left in charge of a household who are surprised when the master returns unexpectedly.

The Story

Who is the faithful and wise servant, charged by his master to manage his household and supply them with food at the proper time? Happy that servant if his master comes home and finds him at work! Truly I tell you: he will be put in charge of all his master's property. But if he is a bad servant and says to himself, "The master is a long time coming," and begins to bully the other servants and to eat and drink with his drunken friends, then the master will arrive on a day when the servant does not expect him, at a time he has not been told. He will cut him in pieces and assign him a place among the hypocrites, where there is wailing and grinding of teeth.'

Comments on the Story

In the Gospel of Matthew, Jesus repeatedly alerts his audiences that he will return as part of a coming cosmic cataclysm that will end this old, broken age and establish the new world in which all things take place in accord with God's design (the reign of God). This cataclysm will be accompanied by the judgment of all people, with some being assigned to eternal perdition while others will enjoy the new world. Matthew 24–25 is the climax of Jesus' teaching on this theme. In 24:1-41, Matthew describes the social and cosmic chaos that will be a part of the collapse of the old world. While this discourse is reported as if Jesus spoke it in the past, Matthew uses it to interpret the conditions of the world in which he wrote the Gospel: the chaos of Matthew's time is the tribulation and suffering expected immediately before the end. Matthew 24:42-44 reminds the listeners that they cannot know the precise time that God will come. But they need to be ready for Jesus' return so that they will be welcomed into God's eternal rule.

The parable of the faithful and unfaithful servants is the first in a catena of four parables that help the church know how to prepare for Jesus' return. All four parables presuppose that the church is in an indefinite time of waiting for the end during which they need to keep awake. As discussed more fully in connection with the parable of the wheat and the darnel (weeds) (Matthew 13:24-

30, 36-43), a catena is a collection of stories on a common theme. Each story contributes something fresh to the theme. The parable of the faithful and unfaithful servants stresses that "keeping awake" is not passive waiting but is working for God. According to the parable of the ten young women awaiting the bridegroom (Matthew 25:1-13), the work is to keep the community's lamp shining "as a light to the Gentiles." The parable of the talents (Matthew 25:14-30) urges the community to let its light shine by expanding its witness even in the midst of difficulty. However, the final story of the separation of the sheep and the goats (Matthew 25:31-46) reveals that Gentiles will be welcomed into God's reign on the basis of their treatment of the "least." The church, of course, will be judged on the degree to which it has "kept awake."

The question at the beginning of the parable provokes the listeners to think about the story as it unfolds. The parable tells of one servant who can choose either to be faithful and wise, or bad.

The designation "wise" is not the usual term, *sophos*, but rather is *phronimos*, a term that is also used to describe the five "wise" young women in Matthew 25:1-13. *Phronimos* refers to the creativity, imagination, and even shrewdness necessary to make one's way through difficult circumstances. Matthew uses the same term in 7:24 to speak of the person "who has the sense" (*phronimos*) to build a house on the rock. That house stands while the house built on the sand falls. Jesus advises the disciples to be "wary" (*phronimos*) as serpents (Matthew 10:16). The servant must be both reliable and clever.

The basic story behind this parable resembles in many respects the popular story of Ahikar, who, according to legend, was a sage and vizier for Sennacherib, king of Assyria. When Ahikar had become old and ready to retire, he passed on his position in the court to his adopted son and nephew, Nadan. "Thus spake Haiqâr [Ahikar], and when he had finished these injunctions and proverbs to Nadan, his sister's son, he imagined that he would keep them all, and he knew not that instead of that he was displaying to him weariness and contempt and mockery.

Thereafter Haiqâr sat still in his house and delivered over to Nadan all his goods, and the slaves, and the handmaidens, and the horses, and the cattle, and everything else that he had possessed and gained; and the power of bidding and of forbidding remained in the hand of Nadan . . . Haiqâr sat at rest in his house, and every now and then Haiqâr went and paid his respects to the king, and returned home. Now when Nadan perceived that the power of bidding and of forbidding was in his own hand, he despised the position of Haiqâr and

The owner is evidently going on an extended trip with an indefinite return date. Such absences were common in the world of the Bible. The auditor in Matthew's day, of course, thinks of Jesus—currently absent but soon to return. One servant is left in charge of the household. The question of the parable is thus particularly directed to leaders in the Christian community awaiting Jesus' return. "Are you a faithful and wise leader?" it asks all such leaders, then and now.

The servant is to manage—to make sure that the other servants perform their responsibilities, to take care of financial affairs, to oversee the buildings and grounds. As a leader, the servant is especially charged to supply the household members (including the other servants) with "food at the proper time." This language is reminiscent of Psalm 104:27. The servant is an agent through whom God intends to mediate divine provision for the community. Indeed, the servant is a means whereby God provides in the communal sphere just as God provides in the cosmic sphere (Matthew 5:45-48; 6:25-34). This theme would be especially important in a community in which some members suffer deprivation (Matthew 8:20; 10:9-10, 40-42; 24:7). As the parable of the sheep and the goats makes clear, the leaders are to provide particularly for "the least" (25:31-46).

scoffed at him, and set about blaming him whenever he appeared, saying, 'My uncle Haiqâr is in his dotage, and he knows nothing now'; and he began to beat the slaves and the handmaidens, and to sell the horses and the camels and be spendthrift with all that his uncle Haiqâr had owned.

And when Haiqâr saw that he had no compassion on his servants nor on his household, he arose and chased him from his house, and sent to inform the king that he had scattered his possessions and his provision.

And the king arose and called Nadan and said to him: 'Whilst Haiqâr remains in health, no one shall rule over his goods, nor over his household, nor over his possessions.' And the hand of Nadan was lifted off from his uncle Haiqâr and from all his goods, and in the meantime he went neither in nor out, nor did he greet him." (*The Story of Ahikar* [Arabic version] 3:1-5 [original story fifth century B.C.E.; many later versions]; from Charles, 2.740-41)

The servant will be "happy" if found "at work" when the owner returns. The English "happy" does not catch the depths intended by the Greek *makarios*. "Happy" is the same word that introduces the beatitudes (Matthew 5:3-11), and in this context refers to the abiding joy that comes with being included in God's rule. "Work" (*poieō*) is a favorite Matthean expression. A person's works can be good or evil. For instance, those who do (*poieō*) the will of God are welcomed into the divine reign. Contrariwise, those who violate God's will are denied a place in God's rule (Matthew 7:21-26; cf. 4:19; 12:33-37; 13:23; 23:3).

The servant who does what the owner asks is put in charge of all the owner's property. This promise is not to be understood as a crass "promotion." For while Jesus promises the twelve that they will sit on twelve thrones (Matthew 19:27-30), he reinterprets this notion: to lead is to empty oneself through service for the sake of others (Matthew 20:20-28).

The bad servant does not fulfill the owner's command. In one of the few windows into the interior life of a character in a parable, the bad servant "says to himself." The English loses an important Matthean echo, for the Greek reads "says in his heart." The heart is the center of the self, from which issues thought, feeling, actions. The undivided heart (the pure heart of Matthew 5:8) seeks to serve God alone. The divided heart does not stay fixed on God, but allows the self to serve its own passions or idols. The fixation of the heart determines one's treasure and its location (6:21). Life actions reveal the condition of the heart (12:34). The evil servant's plot to take advantage of the owner's delay (Matthew 24:48) reveals a divided heart.

The wicked overseer bullies the other servants. Ordinarily the owner either beat a slave directly, or ordered the beating of a slave. A beating was typically administered only for a gross transgression. In a flagrant abuse of power, the wicked slave presumes the prerogative of the owner.

The evil servant then eats and drinks with drunken companions. The contrast with Psalm 104:27 is stark. The faithful and wise servant mediates divine provision for others, while the self-centered wicked slave eats and drinks only with drunken companions. Drunkenness was particularly loathsome because it rendered the self unable to make conscientious moral choices. Drunkenness also led to antisocial behavior, and habitual drunkenness to economic ruin. Biblical speakers (especially in the wisdom tradition) frequently caution the community against becoming drunk (Proverbs 20:1; 21:17; 23:20-21; Amos 6:6; Ecclesiasticus 31:29). Isaiah charges that drunkenness results in moral blindness (5:11-12; 28:1-10). The drunk is preoccupied by immediate sensation and cannot think wisely (*phronimos*) on behalf of the community that they are to lead in preparing for the second coming. Instead, they revert to old-age behavior by squandering their time and resources in self-centered preoccupations.

The owner arrives unexpectedly. The evil servant has no time to clean up the vomit from the revelry. The wicked slave is immediately called to account. There is no time to repent. The owner cuts the slave in pieces. The term "cut in pieces" (*dichotomeō*) is the root of our word "dichotomy." This image creates a powerful visceral reaction in the listener as it recalls the notorious Persian practice of physically dismembering persons. Thematically the image may recall Matthew 18:15-20, where Jesus indicates that some in the community will be excommunicated because they disrupt the common life. Those who are excommunicated are damaged in the same degree as the Persian victims who were dismembered.

The owner then throws the evil servant—who has been a leader in the Christian community—in with the hypocrites. Matthew's fullest description of the hypocrites is 23:1-39, among whom are the blind Pharisees who neglect the weightier matters of the law (justice, mercy, and good faith), who are like whitewashed tombs, and who are condemned to hell. The evil servant and the hypocrites are thrown into the place of eternal wailing and grinding of teeth.

The parable implicitly asks the listener, "Which type of servant will you be: faithful and wise, or evil?" Community leaders are to keep awake in anticipation of Jesus' return by being faithful and wise in mediating God's provisions for all. Those who fail to do so suffer the consequences.

In Luke 12:35-40 Jesus admonishes the disciples to be ready for his return. Peter wants to know if Jesus' teaching is for everyone or especially for the disciples. The parable compares the disciples to the character in the story and, as in the case of Matthew, implicitly asks them to decide whether they want to be like the trusty and sensible steward or the bullying servant. Luke's steward is a step higher on the social ladder than Matthew's servant. A steward manages more of the owner's affairs than the typical servant. Luke adds that the evil steward beats women servants as well as men (12:45).

In an extension of the story, Luke notes that those who know God's will but do not do it will be flogged severely. Those who are ignorant of the divine purposes will be flogged less severely (12:47-48). Peter and the other leaders have been given much; consequently, much is required of them (12:48). The parable thus sends a strong message to the community to be sensible and trustworthy.

Retelling the Story

> "Then the master will arrive on a day when the servant does not expect him, at a time he has not been told." (Matthew 24:50)

"Wait 'til your Dad gets home—you'll really get it then!"

He had heard this warning since he was a kid. And there was a time when it mattered. He remembered all too well those whippings he had gotten as a kid when his dad *did* return home. Bud was always in trouble with his dad for something or other.

But *now* things were different. Bud was all grown up. His dad had left on a long trip and people were thinking he might never return. Bud, as the oldest son, had inherited everything—the family home, the family business, the family trust fund. *Now* Bud was in charge.

Of course, Bud knew exactly what his dad would expect of him. He would expect Bud to do things exactly as he had done. And he would expect everything to be in as good a shape when he returned as it had been when he left, if not better.

But Bud had his own ideas. His dad was too old-fashioned—too much tied to the old ways. Now that he had a free hand, Bud could try out his own ideas. Besides, he had been building up a lot of resentment over the years. It was time for him to assert himself and put his own stamp on the family business.

His father had run the business like a family. That is why there had never been a union among his employees. His father had paid a fair wage with generous benefits. His door had always been open to anyone's complaints or suggestions. He was known as a fair and generous man and morale was high at the company. It was known as a good place to work.

But was it as profitable as it could be? Bud was sure it wasn't. So his first act as the new fully installed CEO was to shake up the structure of the company. He brought in his own people to set up a different management structure, one that demanded more work from fewer employees for less pay and fewer benefits. Many of the longtime employees were laid off. Those who were left were forced to take on more tasks and work overtime just to get the same amount of work done. Bud argued that times were tough and the company needed to be "lean and mean." In truth, it was only lean and mean for the workers. For management, especially the top tier, there were generous raises and benefits.

Bud also decided to diversify. Now that he had created a lean and mean workplace, he had some capital for new investments. New divisions of the company were added by purchasing other, smaller businesses. Each of these was treated to the same "lean and mean" philosophy that Bud had applied to the original family business. Soon they too had downsized their workforce while generously padding the benefits for upper management.

Managing this new restructured and much-enlarged business seemed like a piece of cake as long as new capital could be created by squeezing the workers just a little harder. Even though the morale of the workers took a nosedive, Bud took little notice since it did not affect *his* lifestyle. Even when the profit margin began to dip into the red he was able to cover his losses through "creative accounting."

His company was flying high and Bud was the toast of the town. His lavish parties at his new mansion were always covered in the newspapers. He was on the board of every prestigious agency in town. He was the new golden boy of the industry.

Then things began to fall apart. The new workplace standards that he had installed to get more work out of fewer workers were beginning to have their effect. Their products lost their reputation for quality and sales went way down. Then the "creative accounting" that had been keeping the company afloat fell apart.

It seemed to happen all at once, in one short week. First, the company went bankrupt. Then the IRS showed up and he was indicted for fraud.

Nevertheless, he was determined to overcome all of these setbacks. He was sure that with a good team of lawyers he could beat the court case.

But then all of his contingency plans went up in smoke. For suddenly, out of the blue, his dad walked in the door. And Bud knew then that the jig was up. *(Dennis E. Smith)*

MATTHEW 25:1-13

The Ten Young Women Awaiting the Bridegroom

Jesus compares the coming of the rule of God to the events that take place as a bridegroom arrives at night.

The Story

When the day comes, the kingdom of Heaven will be like this. There were ten girls, who took their lamps and went out to meet the bridegroom. Five of them were foolish, and five prudent; when the foolish ones took their lamps, they took no oil with them, but the others took flasks of oil with their lamps. As the bridegroom was a long time in coming, they all dozed off to sleep. But at midnight there came a shout: "Here is the bridegroom! Come out to meet him." Then the girls all got up and trimmed their lamps. The foolish said to the prudent, "Our lamps are going out; give us some of your oil." "No," they answered; "there will never be enough for all of us. You had better go to the dealers and buy some for yourselves." While they were away the bridegroom arrived; those who were ready went in with him to the wedding banquet; and the door was shut. Later the others came back. "Sir, sir, open the door for us," they cried. But he answered, "Truly I tell you: I do not know you." Keep awake then, for you know neither the day nor the hour.'

Comments on the Story

This parable is the second in a catena that stretches from Matthew 24:45 through 25:46. (On the catena, see my remarks on the parable of the faithful and unfaithful servants, Matthew 24:45-51.) It uses the motif of a wedding banquet to talk about the coming of the rule of God. (On Jewish and early Christian use of this motif, see our discussion of the parable of the wedding feast, Matthew 22:1-14.) The parable is not a pure allegory in that it does not contain an allegorical explanation of each of the elements. But each element calls to mind associations from other Jewish writings, or from other parts of Matthew's story of Jesus.

While we do not have detailed knowledge of first-century wedding customs, we do know that a wedding was a major event in a village. The bride and the groom dressed in special clothing and were bedecked with jewels. The bridegroom even wore a crown. Evidently processions left from the homes of the bride and bridegroom and met in a joyous union, accompanied by musicians and tambourines. The wedding procession traveled all over the village. Often the celebration of a wedding would last several days, and would include a great deal of feasting and dancing. Along the way, the bridegroom went to the bride's home and completed the arrangements for the transfer of the bride's property. Our parable may presume this aspect of the wedding. The negotiations between the bride's father and the bridegroom have taken longer than expected. The bridegroom's arrival for the wedding banquet has been delayed. The young women are waiting to light the way for the bridegroom and to add to the festal quality of the moment.

The listener, of course, recognizes a situation that is parallel to that of the early Christian community. The return of Jesus, the bridegroom, is delayed longer than anticipated. The church is waiting through the night, much as the ten young women wait.

Matthew describes the young women as "virgins" (Greek *parthenoi*, the term from which comes the name of the famous Parthenon). Elsewhere in early Christian literature virginity (as well as other forms of sexual restraint) is commended as a way to help people focus on the things of God in the last days (1 Corinthians 7:25-31; Matthew 19:10-12). The book of Revelation describes the morally faithful as virginal (14:4). On the basis of initial external appearances, all ten of the young women appear to be prepared to greet the bridegroom and the new age. But the parable reveals that deeper discernment is required.

The lamps are probably made of clay and about the size of a cereal bowl, with a fixture on one side to hold a wick. The oil floats in the bowl. Periodically, the wick needs to be trimmed in order for the flame to burn smoothly, brightly, and without excessive smoke.

The image of the lamp prompts the listener to think of Israel's vocation to be the light of the world (Isaiah 42:6-7). The church shares in this vocation (Matthew 5:14). To be light in the world is to show other peoples what God offers, what God asks, and how God wants all people to live. Indeed, the light of the church is its good works (5:16). The church's light is to illumine the manifestation of the rule of God by doing what Jesus says. The lamp is also a symbol of understanding (2 Esdras 14:25).

> The rabbis used oil as an image for the Torah giving light to the world. "Just as oil [gives] life to the world, so too do the words of the Torah [give] life to the world. Just as oil gives light to the world, so too do the words of the Torah give light to the world." (*Midrash R. Deuteronomy* 7:3 [ca. second century C.E.]; from Freedman, 7.134)

Five of the young women are wise. (The term for "wise" is *phronimos*, which is discussed in our interpretation of the parable of the faithful and unfaithful servants, Matthew 24:45-51.) They have practical wisdom—the capacity to live creatively even in the midst of challenging circumstances. Five are foolish. The foolish, especially in the wisdom tradition, are unwilling or unable to discern the divine will. They do not employ (or they lack) the prudence to live wisely. The foolish way ends in destruction (Proverbs 1:32; 10:8; Ecclesiasticus 22:11).

In the ancient world, oil was used in the preparation of food, as a fuel, as a medicine, and for anointing people to particular tasks in the community. Oil will be found in abundance in the rule of God (Joel 2:24; *2 Enoch* 8:5 [recension A]). The providence of God was sometimes represented by oil (1 Kings 17:12-16). And several of the rabbis used oil to represent deeds of love and mercy. The importance of such deeds is accentuated and specified even more in the parable of the sheep and the goats (Matthew 25:31-46).

> Plutarch spoke of "philosophers who urge people to take lessons from them, but give no real instruction or advice; for they are like those who trim the lamps, but fail to pour in oil." ("Precepts of Statecraft" 798B [late first century C.E.]; from Boring-Berger-Colpe, 138, no. 182)

Matthew has prepared the listener for the contrast between the wise and the foolish in 7:24-27. The wise (*phronimos*) person builds a house on the rock by hearing and acting on Jesus' words. The actions of wise people effect aspects of the rule of God in human affairs (Matthew 5:21-48). The wise in the church must often think shrewdly about how best to apply Jesus' teaching in their own situations. The foolish hear Jesus' instructions, but do not act on them. In so doing, they build their house on sand, and the fall of it is great. The five foolish young women are not evil. They are careless. They do not exercise the foresight, discernment, and cleverness necessary to wait for Jesus' return. A primary difference between the wise and the foolish is that the wise have disciplined themselves to understand and enact Jesus' words, whereas the foolish have not.

All the young women sleep while they are awaiting the bridegroom. The parable does not criticize them for sleeping. The bridegroom, after all, is delayed. The ten young women awaken at midnight when the bridegroom comes. As they trim their lamps, the five foolish women realize that they do not have sufficient oil and they ask the five wise ones for some oil. The response of the five wise ones is prudent: if they share their oil with the five foolish women, none will have sufficient oil. While this reply is prudent, it is not fully in the spirit of deeds of love and mercy.

The prudent young women suggest that the foolish ones go to dealers and buy some oil. It may seem strange to contemporary listeners for the wise to suggest that the foolish go to a dealer at midnight. Because a wedding celebration occupied the whole town, and lasted several days, it is conceivable that dealers would be willing to sell oil, even in the middle of the night.

The bridegroom arrives. The wise are welcomed into the marriage feast. We can smell the food and hear the joy and celebration inside the house.

The phrase "and the door was shut" has a terrible finality about it. Listeners can envision the large wooden door closing. We hear the bulky mechanism on the lock as it is pushed shut. The opening and closing of a door is a traditional symbol for divine sovereignty and finality (Isaiah 22:22).

When the five imprudent young women return, they cry out, "Sir, sir, open the door for us." The greeting "Sir, sir," would be better translated, "Lord, Lord," thereby reminding the listener of the same expression in Matthew 7:21. Not all who recognize Jesus and cry out to him, even from within the church, will be welcomed into God's eternal dominion. Jesus excludes even some of the early Christian prophets, exorcists, and miracle workers (7:22-23). Even Christian prophets can be false if they do not point to the fullness of the will of God as revealed through Jesus.

The bridegroom's closing remarks to the five are reminiscent of the words that a rabbi spoke when expelling a student from the rabbi's presence. Matthew 25:13 should not encourage a community to speculate about the time of Jesus' return. As the preceding interpretation makes clear, to "keep awake" is to do what Jesus says by witnessing to the rule of God.

Like several other Matthean parables, this one presumes that the church is a mixed body of wise and foolish. The two groups cannot be distinguished by outward signs. However, the day is coming when they will be separated. In preparation, the parable summons all to be wise. In order to do so, they must keep their flasks filled with oil so that their lamps shine. They must be disciplined in learning what Jesus says and creative in applying it to their own situations. Such discipline and creativity is necessary in a time of waiting, when it is easy to think that one can always wait until tomorrow to obey the divine command. But those who live wisely in the interim between the advents will be welcomed into the final wedding banquet and will not be left huddled outside heaven's closed door.

Retelling the Story

> "While they were away the bridegroom arrived; those who were ready went in with him to the wedding banquet; and the door was shut." (Matthew 25:10)

[*Theo is sitting patiently on a chair, reading a Christian magazine while he waits. A packed suitcase is on the floor near his feet. Another chair is beside him. Sam, looking disheveled and carefree, enters at a quick pace.*]

SAM: Hey, Theo. What are you doing in here? Come on, the game is about to start. The guys are all here.

THEO: No thanks. I'm waiting for Josh.

SAM: Yeah, so are we, but he won't be here for hours, man. What, you've already packed your suitcase? Dude, you are way too uptight.

THEO: He told us he could be here any time this afternoon, he wasn't sure when, but we'd better be ready when he gets here, because he won't be able to wait around.

SAM: You know Josh. He's always late. We have plenty of time.

THEO: If I were you, I'd get my suitcase packed.

SAM: I will after the game. Come on, this is THE GAME! You don't want to miss it.

THEO: I don't want to miss Josh. You know how long we've been planning this trip.

SAM: Yeah, this is going to be so cool. I am so psyched! You know the first thing I'm going to do when we get there?

THEO: You won't be getting there at all if you don't go pack your suitcase.

SAM: Will you relax? Like I said, we have plenty of time.

THEO: I am relaxed. You're the one who's sweating.

SAM: Suit yourself. I'm going to go watch the game.

[*Sam exits. Theo resumes reading his magazine. A phone rings, and Theo answers it.*]

THEO: Hello. Oh, hey Josh. Yeah, got my bags all packed. OK, I'll be here. Bye.

[*Offstage, Sam and the guys cheer at a touchdown. Sam enters in a rush.*]

SAM: Dude, you missed it! We just recovered a fumble on the five-yard line and ran it back for a touchdown!

THEO: Awesome!

SAM: Come on, Theo, you're missing the best game of the season!

THEO: Josh just called. He said he's on his way.

SAM: I am so pumped, man. I've got money riding on this game. Come on, Theo, watch it with us!

THEO: Did you hear what I said? Josh is on his way.

SAM: What?

THEO: Josh is on his way. He'll be here soon.

SAM: Cool. [*Begins to walk back to watch the game.*] You coming?

THEO: No. Josh said to be ready when he gets here. He won't have time to wait. You don't want to miss the flight, do you?

SAM: Come on, we can wait in there. Josh will find us.

THEO: But you haven't even packed your suitcase!

SAM: I'll pack when he gets here! I don't want to miss the game, man!

THEO: You aren't listening. He said to be ready when he gets here.

[*SAM exits, shaking his head. After a few moments, JOSH enters. THEO stands to greet him.*]

THEO: Hey, Josh.

JOSH: Hey, Theo. You all ready?

THEO: Sure am. [*picks up his suitcase*]

JOSH: Where are Sam and the other guys?

THEO: They're watching the game. Want me to go get them?

JOSH: Oh man, we don't have much time. I told you guys to all be waiting and ready to go when I got here. OK, you go see if you can drag them away from the television while I load their luggage in the van.

THEO: Ummmm. There's only one problem.

JOSH: What?

THEO: They haven't packed their bags yet.

JOSH: *What?* You're kidding me.

THEO: I'm not kidding you.

JOSH: Well I don't have time to wait while they pack their bags. They'll just have to try to catch up if they can. Come on, let's go.

[*Exit THEO and JOSH. Just after they leave, Sam runs in, holding an empty suitcase with the lid flying open.*]

SAM: Josh! Josh! Wait up! I . . . Oh, man. He's gone.

[*Offstage, voices cheer at another touchdown. SAM glances that direction, frowning. He slowly drops the suitcase, leaving it at stage center while he sulks off the stage.*]

(Randy Graves)

The Talents

A story about servants entrusted with their master's wealth provides a lesson about discipleship under the rule of God.

The Story

It is like a man going abroad, who called his servants and entrusted his capital to them; to one he gave five bags of gold, to another two, to another one, each according to his ability. Then he left the country. The man who had the five bags went at once and employed them in business, and made a profit of five bags, and the man who had the two bags made two. But the man who had been given one bag of gold went off and dug a hole in the ground, and hid his master's money. A long time afterwards their master returned, and proceeded to settle accounts with them. The man who had been given the five bags of gold came and produced the five he had made: "Master," he said, "you left five bags with me; look, I have made five more." "Well done, good and faithful servant!" said the master. "You have proved trustworthy in a small matter; I will now put you in charge of something big. Come and share your master's joy." The man with the two bags then came and said, "Master, you left two bags with me; look, I have made two more." "Well done, good and faithful servant!" said the master. "You have proved trustworthy in a small matter; I will now put you in charge of something big. Come and share your master's joy." Then the man who had been given one bag came and said, "Master, I knew you to be a hard man: you reap where you have not sown, you gather where you have not scattered; so I was afraid, and I went and hid your gold in the ground. Here it is—you have what belongs to you." "You worthless, lazy servant!" said the master. "You knew, did you, that I reap where I have not sown, and gather where I have not scattered? Then you ought to have put my money on deposit, and on my return I should have got it back with interest. Take the bag of gold from him, and give it to the one with the ten bags. For everyone who has will be given more, till he has enough and to spare; and everyone who has nothing will forfeit even what he has. As for the useless servant, throw him out into the dark, where there will be wailing and grinding of teeth!" '

Comments on the Story

This parable is the third in a catena of four stories in Matthew 24:45–25:46. (On the catena, see my comments on the parable of the faithful and unfaithful servants, Matthew 24:45-51.) The parable of the talents directs the church to multiply its witness during the time of waiting for Jesus to return. Like the parable of the ten young women awaiting the bridegroom, this story is not a complete allegory, though some of its elements provoke allegorical associations.

A person of wealth prepares to go on a long trip. This situation was familiar to many first-century readers as wealthy persons sometimes traveled to distant places for extended periods. In such circumstances, servants were often given considerable authority to manage the owner's affairs.

The hearer immediately discerns similarity between the situation in the story and that of the church: the church is waiting for Jesus to return. However, an aspect of Matthew's theology is in tension with the image. In the parable, the wealthy person is absent. According to Matthew, the risen Jesus is present with the church (1:23; 18:20; 28:20). The divine rule is anticipated in the Christian community through the presence of the risen Jesus. However, that rule is not fully manifest. At the second coming, the divine reign will become cosmic in scope.

Each servant is given a bag (or more) of gold. The traditional term "talent" appears in the Greek, and is the largest sum of money in the ancient world. (In fact, the English use of the word "talent" to refer to one's ability came from the extensive use of this parable in the Middle Ages.) The amount of money given to each servant is fantastic since one talent is worth the wages of a day laborer for fifteen years. Each servant is given a different amount *according to ability*. The servants are not asked to go outside of themselves in their management of the money.

In the owner's absence, the first servant went into business and doubled the number of bags of gold. The parable does not indicate the kind of business, but the story's telling leaves the impression that the servant worked quickly

From the rabbis: "A king had two servants, one of whom loved him and the other feared him. The king went on a long journey. During his long absence, the servant who loved him worked industriously taking care of the garden and the palace, and preparing delicacies for his return. The servant who feared him but did not love him, did not even think about the king during his absence. Finally the king returned, and gave a friendly smile to the first minister, because of all the care he had taken to have things prepared for his return. And the servant rejoiced because the king was pleased. Then the king turned threateningly toward the second servant, who trembled and turned pale. This is the difference between one who loves God and one who fears him; the share of those who love God is doubled." (*Yalqut shim'oni* 267 [date unknown]; from Boring-Berger-Colpe, 231, no. 343) and efficiently. The listener assumes, of course, that the venture requires some risk. The second servant does likewise.

The original hearer would not cast aspersions on the third servant for burying the talent. Burying a talent was the safest way to protect money in those days. Indeed, according to tradition, a person who buried entrusted money was not liable for it. The third servant acts according to accepted standards. The surprise in this parable is the fate of the third servant.

The owner returns and settles accounts. The first two servants are designated "good" and "faithful." These words prompt the listener to think of bearing good fruit and bringing forth good treasure (Matthew 7:17-18; 12:34-35). Those who bear good fruit are those who hear Jesus' words and act on them. For instance, they live according to the rule of God as revealed in 5:21-48. They fulfill Jesus' commission to carry the gospel to the Gentiles (28:16-20).

The owner gives the two servants greater responsibility. This motif seems to me to resonate thematically with Matthew's earlier portrayal of the disciples (who function in the first Gospel as prefigurations of the church). Jesus calls the twelve, invests them with authority, and sends them on missionary journeys. The journeys require considerable risk, for the disciples do not take conventional means of security, such as money. They are persecuted (Matthew 9:35–10:39). However, at the "renewal of all things," they will sit on thrones as judges of Israel (19:27-30). When these servants are invited to enter into the joy of the owner, we hear the "joy" as accompanying the manifestation of God's reign (Matthew 28:8).

The servant who was given one talent was afraid of the owner and consequently hid the talent so that it could be returned. This servant paints the owner as harsh. Indeed, the owner reaps without sowing, and harvests without scattering. Since the listener associates the owner with God, this aspect of the parable is troubling to many contemporary Christians. Should we be afraid of God? Is it fair to depict God as harsh? The owner's capacity to reap without sowing hardly seems a standard to which a conventional servant ought to be held. Contemporary hearers can be helped by recalling three things. First, while the parable is allegorically suggestive, it is not a fully developed allegory. Its details cannot be pressed too far. Second, the owner has not asked the third servant to reap without sowing. The owner holds the servant responsible only for what the servant was asked to do. The last servant's fear does not excuse the servant from acting. Third, the listener remembers that what may seem impossible for mortals is possible for God (Matthew 19:26), who is working within the community.

The owner then takes the one bag of gold from the last servant, and it is turned over to the servant who now has ten bags. The owner describes the servant as "slothful," a term that refers to those who lack the resolve to work. They allow inconvenience to stop them from moving from thought to action (Proverbs 6:6, 9; 20:4; 21:25). The owner explains that to those who have, more will be given. In the Matthean context, this saying is not a general life principle, but refers to responsibilities in the rule of God. Those who have nothing will lose even what they have. Indeed, the one-talent servant is cast into the dark place of weeping and grinding of teeth. This conclusion is especially bracing, for the place of weeping and grinding of teeth is also the destination of the evildoers, the improperly clothed guest, the hypocrites, and the unfaithful servant (Matthew 8:12; 13:42, 50; 22:13; 23:29-33; 24:51). The third servant tried to protect the one talent, but that was insufficient.

The parable urges the Christian community to respond to God's rule in the pattern of the first two servants. God wants the church to increase the radius of the shining of its light of good works and testimony. The story of Jesus—who was rejected, crucified, and resurrected—demonstrates the trustworthiness of God toward those who take risks to witness to the divine rule. Ironically, the servants who seek to save their lives will lose them, while those who risk much for God will save their lives (Matthew 16:24-26).

The parallel version of the story in Luke 19:11-27 is also in a context in which Jesus discusses the coming of the divine reign (19:11). The parable concludes Jesus' journey to Jerusalem. Luke recasts the story. The owner is now a noble person seeking royal power. Luke reduces the extravagant talent to the pound (about three months of salary for a day worker). The person of nobility gives one pound each to ten servants and departs. Upon returning, and now in receipt of royal power, the first three servants are called forward. The first, who has taken one pound and made it ten, is congratulated and given responsibility over ten cities. The second, who has made five pounds, is given leadership over five cities.

The third servant has not buried the pound, but has only wrapped it in a cloth (in which case it could easily have been stolen, and for which the servant is liable). The owner commands the one pound to be taken away. The story ends brutally as the person of nobility orders the slaughter of all enemies, which may refer to the destruction of Jerusalem. The listener of Luke's narrative knows that Jerusalem was destroyed in 70 C.E. This text suggests that God ordered (or permitted) the sack of the city because its leaders were one-pound people. According to Luke, when Jesus entered Jerusalem, the leaders did not embrace the way in which he was expanding God's rule (especially toward the Gentile world). They tried to cling to their pound by killing Jesus. In so doing, they brought about the destruction of two of their most potent symbols—Jerusalem and the temple. Christians who wish to avoid a similar fate should model their witness on the behavior of the first two servants.

Retelling the Story

> "It is like a man going abroad, who called his servants and entrusted his capital to them; to one he gave five bags of gold, to another two, to another one, each according to his ability." (Matthew 25:14-15a)

I'm writing a novel. I know you find that hard to believe considering I'm so young and since I am such a dummy. No, my parents don't call me that, and my teacher doesn't call me that, but I know it and that's all that counts. I'm calling the novel *The Curse of the Gifted Sisters*. In the book there is a family with three daughters, kind of like ours. The first daughter is really smart. The second daughter is really good at sports. The third daughter is not really good at anything. The third daughter is the one who is telling the story.

Rabbi Eleazar once counseled one whose son had died: "Rabbi Eleazar entered, sat down before him, and said to him: 'I shall tell thee a parable: to what may this be likened? To a man with whom the king deposited some object. Every single day the man would weep and cry out, saying: "Woe unto me! when shall I be quit of this trust in peace?" Thou too, master, thou hadst a son: he studied the Torah, the Prophets, the Holy Writings, he studied Mishnah, Halakha, Agada, and he departed from the world without sin. And thou shouldst be comforted when thou hast returned thy trust unimpaired.'" (*Avot of Rabbi Nathan* 14 [third–fourth centuries C.E.; compilation seventh–ninth centuries C.E.]; from Goldin, 77)

The first daughter, that is, the oldest one, makes straight A's from first grade through high school. She is in all the "gifted" classes and goes to special schools for "gifted" kids. Every time people come over to her house her parents want her to play the piano (which she is really good at) or recite some poem (which she is also really good at) or something. She's a member of every honor society you ever heard of and a few that nobody has ever heard of. She gets into an Ivy League college on the first try, and to top it off they give her a "full academic scholarship" to go there. To make things worse she is really pretty and is always doing nice things for people. In other words, she is the kind of sister it would be easy to hate.

The second daughter is not as smart as the first one, but she does pretty well in school. She is not gifted or anything but she makes good grades and stays out of trouble. All in all she is pretty ordinary—except when it comes to sports. When she was just a kid she was on the soccer team and softball team in our (I mean, her) neighborhood. Then when she gets to high school she plays basketball in the fall and runs track in the spring. Then she plays softball in the summer, and would play soccer too, if the season didn't conflict with her practices for her other sports. Her room is so full of trophies that she has to step over them and hang her clothes on them just to have room to move. Half the trophies at the middle school have her name on them, and I think they are going to have to buy a new trophy case to hold all the ones she has won already in high school. And she is not even a senior yet. There are already colleges sending people to watch her play and run, and it looks like she is going to have her pick of athletic scholarships wherever she decides to go. She's another sister that's easy to hate.

Then there is the youngest daughter, who is not really good at anything. She doesn't make good grades like the oldest sister. She tried for a while and made mostly B's and C's with an A mixed in every now and again. Then, finally, she just quit trying. She could never live up to her "gifted" sister in the grade department, so why even try? Now she makes C's and D's with a few F's mixed in.

She's not very good at sports either. She has tried just about everything: soccer, softball, basketball, track—but she is just a klutz at everything. Compared to her sister she looks like an old lady out there trying to play soccer or basketball. She was pretty good at softball, but didn't like to practice, so she quit. She was also pretty good at the clarinet, which is something neither of her sisters could play. But she didn't like to practice that either. Sometimes I wonder if she really hates to practice, or if she is just scared that she will never be really good, even if she did practice.

Her teacher tells her she has a good imagination, but she just needs more discipline. And she does like to write stories—like this novel about her, I mean, these sisters. Her parents say she is not living up to her "potential." How do they know what kind of potential she has? They're too busy taking her sisters to visit colleges and to games and award banquets. What do they know about their stupid daughter, the one who is not gifted?

So this youngest sister is going to run away. That will make them all really sorry. Or maybe it won't. Maybe she is too dumb to be missed. Maybe they will be glad she's gone. Anyway she is going to run away and write this novel about her sisters, if she ever gets it together. *(Michael E. Williams)*

The Sheep and the Goats

At the last judgment, the sheep (the righteous) are separated from the goats (the unrighteous) on the basis of their care for those in need.

The Story

When the Son of Man comes in his glory and all the angels with him, he will sit on his glorious throne, with all the nations gathered before him. He will separate people into two groups, as a shepherd separates the sheep from the goats; he will place the sheep on his right hand and the goats on his left. Then the king will say to those on his right, "You have my Father's blessing; come, take possession of the kingdom that has been ready for you since the world was made. For when I was hungry, you gave me food; when thirsty, you gave me drink; when I was a stranger, you took me into your home; when naked, you clothed me; when I was ill, you came to my help; when in prison, you visited me." Then the righteous will reply, "Lord, when was it that we saw you hungry and fed you, or thirsty and gave you drink, a stranger and took you home, or naked and clothed you? When did we see you ill or in prison, and come to visit you?" And the king will answer, "Truly I tell you: anything you did for one of my brothers here, however insignificant, you did for me." Then he will say to those on his left, "A curse is on you; go from my sight to the eternal fire that is ready for the devil and his angels. For when I was hungry, you gave me nothing to eat; when thirsty, nothing to drink; when I was a stranger, you did not welcome me; when I was naked, you did not clothe me; when I was ill and in prison, you did not come to my help." And they in their turn will reply, "Lord, when was it that we saw you hungry or thirsty or a stranger or naked or ill or in prison, and did nothing for you?" And he will answer, "Truly I tell you: anything you failed to do for one of these, however insignificant, you failed to do for me." And they will go away to eternal punishment, but the righteous will enter eternal life.'

Comments on the Story

This story is the last in the catena that stretches from Matthew 24:45 through 25:46. (On the catena, see the comments on the faithful and unfaithful servants, Matthew 24:45-51.) The parable of the sheep and the goats is the crescendo of Jesus' teaching about the final judgment at the time that the old world ends and the new world (God's reign) is implemented in its fullness. Earlier stories have concentrated on the judgment of the Christian community, but this narrative reminds the reader that the entire human family will stand before God. Scholars offer many different interpretations of this passage. I believe that the story offers criteria of judgment that make it possible for persons both inside and outside of Judaism and Christianity to be included (and excluded) in God's reign.

The parable makes use of an everyday shepherding practice. At nightfall, a shepherd tending a herd of sheep and goats would separate the two. The sheep prefer to spend the night in the open air, whereas goats like the warmth of a shelter. The story presumes (as was customary in the first century) that sheep are more valuable than goats.

The scene is the cosmic courtroom after the Son of Man (Jesus) and his angels have defeated Satan and his angels. (On the "Son of Man," see the comments on the wheat and the darnel, Matthew 13:24-30, 36-43.) In addition, this passage describes Jesus as shepherd, a description that evokes not only separation of sheep and goats, but also tender care for the sheep and rebuke of those who would destroy the flock (Psalm 23; Ezekiel 34:11-31). (For more on the shepherd motif, see our discussion of the parable of the lost sheep, Matthew 18:10-14.) Jesus is also monarch, a depiction that is especially suited to this passage. For in Israel, the sovereign was God's agent through whom justice (relationships that manifest God's intention) was to be enacted in the community, especially for the poor, the needy, the weak, and the oppressed (Psalm 72). Matthew thus creates a collage by which we are to understand Jesus as the Son of Man/shepherd/sovereign.

Jesus will render the ultimate verdict on "all the nations." Who is included in the "nations"? In this context, "nations" does not refer to political entities, but to individuals from a wide spectrum of the human family. Scholars debate the extent of the spectrum. Some scholars think it includes all people—Jewish people, Gentiles, the church. Others think the expression refers to non-Christians, whether Gentile or Jewish. Still others take the phrase to refer only to Gentiles. I have space only to summarize why I think the first response is most satisfactory. The church is certainly included, for in the preceding parables, Matthew has been pointing to the judgment of the church, a body that includes both Christian Jews and Gentile Christians, weeds and wheat, bad fish and good, faithful servants and slothful. Matthew's criteria for judgment (the treatment of the least) were already known in the Jewish community; through the identification of Christ with the least, these criteria are now applicable to Christians and, by implication, to all in the human family. Matthew does not insist that all persons become Christian in order to be a part of God's dominion. Indeed, while Matthew is critical of the practice of certain Jewish people of his day (Matthew 23:1-36), the Gospel writer is quite sympathetic to Judaism per se (note Matthew's positive evaluation of the law in 5:17-20; cf. 23:2-3, 23). Matthew gives no indication that Jewish people would be excluded from God's dominion because they are not Christian.

The parable of the sheep and the goats portrays Jewish people being judged on the basis of traditional Jewish criteria (adapted slightly). The parable portrays Gentiles being judged by similar standards. On the latter point, Matthew's thinking may be part of a concern to identify the righteous among the Gentiles that became more widespread in subsequent Judaism. The parable reveals that God is truly righteous, for it provides criteria by which all peoples may be judged equitably.

Jesus sends the sheep to the right of the throne, and the goats to the left. The right side is the preferred one in antiquity (Psalm 110:1). The presence of the terms "blessed" and "cursed" reminds the reader that Jewish covenantal theology lies behind this scene: the obedient are blessed, while the disobedient are cursed. In this context, the blessed are welcomed into God's eternal dominion; the cursed are sent to eternal fire. Jesus says that God's rule "has been ready for you since the world was made." This statement is not an arbitrary doctrine of predestination. The behavior and attitudes of the sheep and the goats in the old age set the course for their ultimate destination.

The criteria by which the sheep are identified derive from the concern for the marginalized that permeates Jewish tradition. The community that is obedient to God's will provides for the vulnerable, and is blessed. The disobedient community is cursed because it does not provide for the poor (Deuteronomy 27–28, esp. 27:18-19; cf. Ezekiel 22:6-12; Malachi 3:5). Jewish tradition specifically directs the attention of the community to five of the six difficulties mentioned in this passage: hunger, thirst, being a stranger, nakedness, and illness (Job 31:32; Isaiah 58:6-10; Ezekiel 18:5-9, 14-18; Tobit 4:16; Ecclesiasticus 4:1-6; 7:32-35; 2 Esdras 2:20-24; *Testament of Joseph* 1:5-7). Matthew earlier echoes this tradition in 9:13; 12:7; 22:34-40; 23:23. Later rab-

> The theme of care for the poor is omnipresent in the rabbinical writings. "*Open to me the gates of righteousness* (Psalm 118:19). When a man is asked in the world-to-come: 'What was thy work?' and he answers: 'I fed the hungry,' it will be said to him: '*This is the gate of the Lord* (Psalm 118:20). Enter into it, O thou that didst feed the hungry.'
>
> When a man answers: 'I gave drink to the thirsty,' it will be said to him: '*This is the gate of the Lord.* Enter into it, O thou that didst give drink to the thirsty.'
>
> When a man answers: 'I clothed the naked,' it will be said to him: '*This is the gate of the Lord.* Enter into it, O thou that didst clothe the naked.'
>
> This will be said also to him that brought up the fatherless, and to them that gave alms or performed deeds of loving-kindness." (*Midrash on Psalms* 118:19 [ca. ninth century C.E.]; from Braude, *Psalms*, 2.243)

binic literature designates these as "acts of kindness." In the parable, they represent the full range of vulnerabilities. The sheep are now described as the "righteous," a term that Matthew uses for people who both hear and do what God asks (1:19; 3:15; 5:6; 7:21-27; 10:41; 13:17; 23:29, 34). The sheep live rightly in the world by ministering to the hungry, thirsty, strangers, naked, sick, and imprisoned. In essence, the sheep take the role of shepherds in behalf of the needy.

Jesus, the sovereign cosmic judge, identifies with the needy: "For when *I* was hungry, you gave me food . . . ." The righteous do not recall directly serving Jesus. Hence, he clarifies, "Anything you did for one of my brothers here, however insignificant, you did for me." Most scholars think that the needy in this parable are early Christian witnesses. Scholars come to this conclusion because Jesus' "brothers" are those who do the will of God (Matthew 12:46-50; cf. Matthew 28:10). Further, Jesus explicitly describes his followers as "little ones" (Matthew 10:42; 18:6, 10, 14). (The Greek rendered "insignificant" in the REB is a form of the term "little ones.") Jesus tells his followers that they will experience conditions similar to those of Matthew 25:35-36 when they make their witness, especially during the tribulation (Matthew 10:16-37; 24:4-7, 9-28). As the name Emmanuel indicates, Jesus is present with the community in its suffering (Matthew 1:23; cf. 18:20; 28:20). As Jesus says to the disciples as they set out on their missionary journeys, "To receive you is to receive me, and to receive me is to receive the One who sent me" (10:40).

Jesus speaks this parable in Matthew 25. In Matthew 26–27, he is betrayed, rejected, and killed. He becomes the paradigm of the insignificant—homeless, thirsty, imprisoned. The listener, however, recognizes that in Jesus' apparent defeat, the will of God is at work to bring the new age. The Gospel of Matthew sees Jesus as a mode of the divine presence in the world (1:23; 18:20; 28:19). The parable interprets Jesus' solidarity with the poor as one aspect of that presence.

The identification of the "insignificant" with early Christian witnesses raises a potential theological difficulty for the preacher, teacher, or storyteller. Are the peoples of the world to be judged on the degree to which they serve Christians? Such a conclusion would reverse Christian intention. According to Matthew, the church is a light in the world (Matthew 5:14). To use contemporary language, the church *represents* God's presence and purposes. In Matthew's day, Christians sometimes encountered resistance to their witness that left them hungry, thirsty, homeless, inadequately clothed, sick, and in occasional trouble with authorities. Their fate *represents* the needy of the world. The powers of the present age resist God's will for justice and God's new world. The goats—rulers of the current world—ignore or mistreat the poor. To serve the needy is to join God's dissatisfaction with the present age; it is to resist the powers that profit from the poor and that keep the poor in poverty; it is to embody God's will in the new age for all to be fed, housed, clothed, healthy, and free.

Jesus' presence with the poor of the Christian community represents Jesus' presence with all the suffering of the world. At one level, God's presence with the poor means that God feels the pain of poverty, and is empathetic and comforting. At another level, the Jewish affirmation that God is with the community means not only that God shares in the community's sorrow, joy, and common life, it also means that God will act to make the community's situation right (Exodus 3:12; Isaiah 43:1-7, esp. v. 2). The listener who hears that Emmanuel is with the vulnerable understands that affirmation as also a promise that God will act to conform the world to God's purposes.

The sheep are declared righteous because they actively provide for the needs of the vulnerable. The goats are sent into eternal fire because they did not.

The parable does not directly suggest that one must become Christian in order to be welcomed into the sovereignty that was made ready before the world began. Jewish people, evidently, are declared righteous, and are welcomed into the eternal divine orb on the basis of criteria that are as old as their own tradition. The Jewish person who tends to the poor mirrors God's concern. Gentiles, too, can be declared righteous and can be received into God's domain because they recognize that poverty is undesirable and they take steps to see that the poor are fed, clothed, and housed. While they have not had the advantage of the special revelation given to the Jewish community, they have been able to discern from nature, conscience, and other general sources of revelation that the Transcendent Power of the Universe does not will marginalization and suffering.

In Matthew, the parable is intended to motivate Christian listeners to care for the poor. The story undercuts Christian arrogance by reminding the community that the righteous are found among Jewish people and even among unbelieving Gentiles. The immediately previous parables suggest that some Christians will be goats.

The narrative reminds the reader that God is present even among the people whom the world designates "insignificant," and that Christians (and others) are accountable for their behavior toward them. The parable is also a stinging critique on communities that allow hunger, homelessness, nakedness, and violence. They deny themselves opportunities for blessing and invoke the curse on their common life. Indeed, those who allow this present life to be a time of suffering for the poor will find that the suffering of the poor is pale beside the "eternal fire that is ready for the devil."

This parable does not advocate works-righteousness. Works-righteousness is the idea that one must accomplish certain works in order to be welcomed into the circle of God's love. God has graciously revealed God's love for all and God's will for justice in the world. This revelation bestows identity upon the community, an identity that includes acting in solidarity with the poor. The sheep enact who they are and what God has called them to do, whereas the goats deny who they are. Acts of mercy for others respond to the mercy that God shows for us. Those who refuse to act compassionately toward the poor refuse God's compassion for them and for the world.

Retelling the Story

> "He will separate people into two groups, as a shepherd separates the sheep from the goats." (Matthew 25:32b)

During the fourth century, after the time of Jesus, men and women began to form communities in the desert in Egypt. It had become more and more difficult for these men and women to live out their faith in a church that was now the state church of the Roman Empire. Since his conversion to the Christian faith the emperor had called church councils together and ratified their decisions. Bishops and priests began to take on the dress of the rich and powerful members of society.

So some Christians of that time decided to leave the cities and towns of the empire and create a new kind of community in the desert. They would fast and pray, support themselves by their work, and learn "to love the way God loves." They lived in small dwellings called cells. Many of these woman and men were singular characters, and soon stories began to circulate about them. The stories were far more than entertainment, however. After a while these stories became a means of teaching others about the life of the desert and the Christians who lived there. In short, they became what we today would call stories of spiritual formation. Many of these stories were collected in books and a number of translations of them exist today.

Though all of the stories reflected lives that were based on the scriptures, especially the teachings of Jesus, not all of them mention stories or passages from the Bible directly. On the other hand, others of these stories seem to be intended to interpret biblical texts. I think you'll recognize the passage to which the following story refers.

Once there was a brother who was known to be adept at casting out demons and other unclean spirits that sometimes afflicted people. One day the brother was called to exorcise an evil spirit from a young man who lived in a nearby village. As the brother approached the young man the evil spirit began to groan like a wild animal. "What do you want with me?" the spirit asked through the young man's clenched teeth. The young man's body was nothing but skin and bones as the resident spirit sapped him of all that makes one healthy and human.

"I have come to try to convince you to leave the body of this poor soul and never to return to torment him, or anyone else again," the brother replied.

"And just how do you propose to do that?" the evil spirit said. He spat as he spoke and finished his question with a terrifying laugh.

"Oh, it will not be me who sends you away. I do not have the power to do that. It will be Jesus who will send you away." The brother tried to hold on to some semblance of inner peace while facing this terrible creature in the body of the poor fellow who stood before him racked with pain.

"Speaking of Jesus, I have a proposition for you." It was not unusual for a demon to demand some concession for leaving the body of a human.

"What is that?" asked the brother.

"I have always been puzzled by one story that this Jesus told, and I want you to explain it to me." The evil spirit sounded almost reasonable now.

"I am no scholar, but I will offer what help I can," the brother quietly replied.

"If you are able to answer my question I will leave the body of this young man immediately," the demon said.

"And never return?" the brother asked.

"And never return," the spirit promised.

"To him or anyone else?" the brother persisted.

"Oh, very well, I will leave and never possess another human soul, but that is only if you can answer the question to my satisfaction." A smile that was more like a grimace crossed the face of the young man.

"As I said, I will try," the brother offered.

"Oh, I can tell that you are a very holy man," the demon sneered. "You should have no problem with this one. Tell me, in the parable Jesus told about the Last Judgment, who are the sheep and who are the goats? It seems to me that all of you holy people think you are the chosen ones, and others are to be sent packing. Tell me, who are they, really?"

The brother was quiet for a very long time. "I do not know," the brother admitted. The evil spirit laughed a terrible laugh. "But," the brother continued, "I can tell you what I do know for a fact. You see, I do know that I am one of the goats. As for the sheep, they are known only to God."

Hearing that, the demon gave an awful shriek and left the body of the young man, screaming, "It is not your answer but your humility that has driven me out."

They say that the brother stayed and cared for the young man until he was well and strong enough to care for himself. *(Michael E. Williams)*

> To some of the rabbis, deeds of help for the impoverished are more important than sacrifice. "R. Eleazar stated, Greater is he who performs charity than [he who offers] all the sacrifices, for it is said, *To do charity and justice is more acceptable to the Lord than sacrifice.*" (*b. Sukkah* 49b [ca. sixth century C.E.]; from Epstein, 8.233)

LUKE 10:25-37

The Compassionate Samaritan

A Samaritan, who shows neighbor-love to the victim of a robbery left alongside the road, demonstrates the inclusivity of the domain of God.

The Story

A lawyer once came forward to test him by asking: 'Teacher, what must I do to inherit eternal life?' Jesus said, 'What is written in the law? What is your reading of it?' He replied, 'Love the Lord your God with all your heart, and with all your soul, and with all your strength, and with all your mind; and your neighbour as yourself.' 'That is the right answer,' said Jesus; 'do that and you will have life.'

Wanting to justify his question, he asked, 'But who is my neighbour?' Jesus replied, 'A man was on his way from Jerusalem down to Jericho when he was set upon by robbers, who stripped and beat him, and went off leaving him half dead. It so happened that a priest was going down by the same road, and when he saw him, he went past on the other side. So too a Levite came to the place, and when he saw him went past on the other side. But a Samaritan who was going that way came upon him, and when he saw him he was moved to pity. He went up and bandaged his wounds, bathing them with oil and wine. Then he lifted him on to his own beast, brought him to an inn, and looked after him. Next day he produced two silver pieces and gave them to the innkeeper, and said, "Look after him; and if you spend more, I will repay you on my way back." Which of these three do you think was neighbour to the man who fell into the hands of the robbers?' He answered, 'The one who showed him kindness.' Jesus said to him, 'Go and do as he did.'

Comments on the Story

While Luke 10:25-28 is not part of the parable, it is important for understanding the parable. The lawyer, an interpreter of the law, voices a question that stirs in the hearts of listeners today: "What must I do to inherit eternal life?" In this setting, "eternal life" refers not just to individual survival in an afterlife, but also to participation in the dominion of God. Jesus, in a style of response that was characteristic of rabbis of the time, replies with questions. The lawyer turns to scripture and joins Deuteronomy 6:5 (love of God) and Leviticus 19:18 (love of neighbor). By the first century, other Jewish leaders also conjoined these two texts to express the essence of Judaism (see, for example, Philo; *Testament of Issachar* 5:2; *Testament of Dan* 5:3). Love for

God is incomplete until one loves the neighbor. Neighbor-love is a part of expressing love for God. Love for God creates a community of neighbors who practice love for one another.

The lawyer desires to "justify his question," i.e., to be sure that the answer is clear. The lawyer asks, "Who is my neighbour?" The lawyer wants to know whom to love in order to be included in the rule of God. The parable of the compassionate Samaritan reframes the issue by causing the lawyer (and the listener) to consider another question: Who exercises neighbor-love and, therefore, is included in the dominion of God? By reframing the question, Luke helps prepare the hearer for the fact that in his second volume, the book of Acts, the Christian community includes both Jewish people and Gentiles. The inclusiveness of the church prefigures the inclusive community of the last age. Of course, the parable also encourages hearers to want to be neighbors.

> According to Hillel, all a non-Jew [like the Samaritan] needed to know about the law was contained in the Golden Rule: "On another occasion it happened that a certain heathen came before Shammai and said to him, 'Make me a proselyte, on condition that you teach me the whole Torah while I stand on one foot.' Thereupon he repulsed him with the builder's cubit which was in his hand. When he went before Hillel, he said to him, 'What is hateful to you, do not to your neighbour: that is the whole Torah, while the rest is the commentary thereof; go and learn it.'" (*b. Shabbat* 31a [Hillel: first century C.E.; text: ca. sixth century C.E.]; from Epstein, 3.140)

The story tells of a traveler who is simply identified as "a man." This open-ended expression encourages the listener to identify with the traveler. I imagine myself going down the road from Jerusalem to Jericho. The distance is about seventeen miles, and the road is literally "down" since Jerusalem is 3,200 feet higher in elevation than Jericho. The road is winding. In antiquity, robbers frequently hid among rocks and cliffs along the side and ambushed travelers. The mention of this particular road strikes a chord of fear in the hearer.

The robbers leave the traveler beaten, naked, and half-dead. In the ancient world, a person's racial and ethnic identity was indicated by clothing and by language and speech patterns. The victim is naked and cannot talk. Neither the characters in the story, nor the listeners of the story, know the specific identity of the victim. The traveler is pictured as a case of extreme human need. As listeners, we feel what it is like to be in the ditch.

A priest and a Levite come down the road. Why are they going from Jerusalem to Jericho? Many temple functionaries lived in Jericho. They commuted between Jerusalem and Jericho, serving at the temple for two weeks, then returning home. Likely, these two characters are on the way home.

Christian preachers have given the priest and the Levite a beating that overlooks the seriousness and complexity of their situations. According to the Torah, a priest may have contact only with the corpse of a direct relative; contact with any other corpse defiles a priest and renders the priest unclean (Leviticus 21:1-4; cf. Numbers 5:1-4; 19:1-22; 31:19-24; Ezekiel 44:25-27). In order to be cleansed and readied for temple service, the priest must perform the complicated ceremony of the red heifer (Numbers 19:1-22). Furthermore, the priest has no income from the temple during the time of uncleanness. Consequently, the priest's family and larger household are left vulnerable. In a sense, the priest is caught between love for God as expressed through obedience to the Torah, and a practical expression of love for neighbor. The text says that the victim is half-dead. But from a distance, the victim may look dead.

The Levites performed lesser services at the temple than the priests. Like the priest, contact with a corpse leaves the Levite unclean.

Many ancient stories involved three characters, the third of which is usually a hero or heroine. In this parable, the expected sequence would be a priest (religious professional), a Levite (a religious professional but not as highly regarded as the priest), and an ordinary Israelite. But instead, the listener is stunned by the identity as well as the behavior of the Samaritan. Today's storyteller might try to create the sound of shock in the telling of the story.

The Samaritans were originally part of the Jewish family. They lived in Samaria, a territory north of Jerusalem. But while the Jewish leadership was exiled in Babylonia, the Samaritans who remained in Palestine developed their own religious life. Of course, they were monotheistic. They adopted the five books of Moses as their only scriptures. They identified Mt. Gerizim as their sacred mountain and built a temple on it. They developed their own priesthood and many distinct customs. When the exiles returned, the Samaritans decried the restoration of the temple at Jerusalem. Two centuries before Jesus, they assisted the Syrians in a campaign against the Jewish people. In the preceding century, the Jewish people had burned Samaritan holy places on Mt. Gerizim. In their campaign with the Syrians, the Samaritans reciprocated by scattering the bones of a corpse in the temple in Jerusalem and thus rendering it unfit for the Passover celebration. Ecclesiasticus summarized Jewish feeling toward Samaritans in this way: "Two nations I detest, and a third is no nation at all: the inhabitants of Mount Seir, the Philistines, and the senseless folk that live at Shechem [i.e., the Samaritans]" (50:25-26).

Luke earlier had invoked this prejudice against Samaritans by mentioning that they did not receive the messengers of Jesus (9:51-56). Luke later calls attention to the extent of God's love by saying that the gospel will be preached in Samaria (Acts 1:8). A successful mission to Samaria is described in Acts 8:5-25.

In the parable, the Samaritan is "moved to pity." The Greek word for "pity" refers to the "inward parts," or the "bowels." In Jewish thought, the bowels are the center of feeling (Proverbs 12:10; 17:5; Ecclesiasticus 30:7; 33:5; 4 Maccabees 14:13), and even the center of mercy (*Testament of Zebulon* 5:3-4). Indeed, in the last days (a theme close to Luke's heart: Acts 2:17), "God will send his compassion on the earth, and whenever he finds compassionate mercy, in that person he will dwell" (*Testament of Zebulon* 8:2; cf. 8:6). In the parable, the term is part of a compound word that emphasizes "feeling with another." (The same is true of the English word *compassion*: *passion* [to feel suffering] + *com* [with].) In the Jewish tradition, God is the great exemplar for feeling the sufferings of others (Exodus 3:7-8). The Samaritan feels the desperation of the person alongside the road, and stops to help. The Samaritan may remember the feeling of being "passed by" (as a result of prejudice) in social dealings with other persons. Hence, another surprise for the hearer: the pain of the Samaritan becomes a source of healing power.

The Samaritan's first action is to bathe the victim's wounds with wine (an astringent for disinfecting) and oil (a balm to ease the pain) and to bandage them. The listener who is familiar with the Jewish tradition, however, hears additional echoes. God binds up the wounds of Zion (Jeremiah 30:17; Hosea 6:1). Other reverberations are prompted by the preceding emphasis on love of God and love of neighbor. Wine and oil were used as libations as part of the sacrifices offered at the temple. The listener hears the Samaritan's use of them as almost an act of worship, thus uniting love of God and love of neighbor in a single act. Even though the Samaritans do not recognize the validity of the prophetic books, this Samaritan fulfills the prophetic hope for worship to eventuate in lives of justice and mercy (Hosea 6:6; Micah 6:7-8).

The Samaritan puts the wounded traveler on his beast and leads the beast to an inn. The fact that the Samaritan has a beast (and is not walking) indicates that the Samaritan is in the middle class or upper class. Further, in that time persons of lower social status typically led the animals of persons of higher social status. The Samaritan embodies the social reversal that takes place in the rule of God as rulers become servants (Luke 22:24-27; cf. 6:20-26; 9:22-27).

The Samaritan takes the wounded traveler to an inn and makes financial arrangements for the care of the victim. This step is important, for if the victim is unable to pay the bill, the victim will be arrested. The Samaritan's deposit and promise ensure the victim's freedom.

Jesus simultaneously asks the lawyer, and the listener to the story, which of the three characters proved to be neighbor to the person who fell into the hands of robbers. The answer is self-evident: the person who showed kindness. Showing kindness for another is at the center of the nature of God (Exodus 34:6-7; Psalm 86:15; 103:8; Jeremiah 32:18; Hosea 11:1-11; Jonah 4:2), and it is the epitome of Jewish ethics (Exodus 2:6; Psalm 72:13; Proverbs 21:10;

Ezekiel 16:5; Amos 1:11; Zechariah 7:9-10). Indeed, the Greek word rendered "kindness" or "mercy" (*eleos*) is the term used by the Greek Bible, the Septuagint, to translate the important Hebrew term *hesed*, the "faithful loving-kindness" of God. The Samaritan is the means through whom the divine *hesed* is mediated to the person in the ditch.

At one level, Jesus' closing admonition ("Go . . .") makes the story an example for the lawyer and the listener. We, too, should express love for God and love for neighbor by responding with compassion to the victims alongside the road of life. We ourselves may someday need the Samaritan's neighbor-love. At another level, the parable challenges all our narrow prejudices and tribal boundaries. The story invites us to enlarge our vision of the boundaries of the rule of God. If God can welcome (and work through) Samaritans, then so should the church. Jesus makes this theme explicit by commissioning the church to witness "throughout all Judaea and Samaria, and even in the farthest corners of the earth" (Acts 1:8; 8:1, 4-25; see also Luke 24:47). So also today, the Christian community may need to leave its ghetto and join the Samaritans of the world in loving God and neighbor.

Retelling the Story

> "Which of these three do you think was neighbour to the man who fell into the hands of the robbers?" (Luke 10:36)

A religious scholar came to a rabbi one day and asked, "What must I do to find favor with God?"

> Like Jesus, the rabbis also emphasized the importance of compassion for the needy, as seen in this story: "It is related of Nahum of Gamzu that he was blind in both his eyes, his two hands and legs were amputated, and his whole body was covered with boils and he was lying in a dilapidated house on a bed the feet of which were standing in bowls of water in order to prevent the ants from crawling on to him. . . . His disciples said to him, Master, since you are wholly righteous, why has all

"You're the scholar," the rabbi replied. "What do you read in the Bible?"

"Love God and your neighbor would be a pretty good summary," the religious scholar responded with confidence.

"You are right," the rabbi told him. "Just try to do those two things."

"There is something I have never been quite clear on," the scholar continued. "Who exactly is my neighbor?"

At that the rabbi told this story.

Once a traveling evangelist was going from Charlotte, North Carolina, to the Holy Land. He had traveled there many times before and so approached the trip with little hesitancy. He had first traveled there with his father, who had also crossed the globe bringing the word of God to poor benighted humanity. The son had been invited back to speak there because of some comments he had made that were quoted in the *Jerusalem Post*. For years the younger evangelist had been on a crusade to convert the Jews, believing that these conversions would hasten the second coming of Jesus. This meant that he had not always been welcomed by Jewish communities in his home country or in Israel.

"The Jews and the Christians worship the same God, though we have very different ways of worshiping him," read the quote. "But the God of Islam is NOT the same God as the one we worship. In fact, the God of the Muslims is a god of hatred and vengeance, of homicide bombers who murder innocent children."

Now he was on his way. He had stopped off for a preaching engagement in Chicago and was walking back to the rental car he would drop off at O'Hare. From an alley emerged three shady characters who began to follow him. He could hear them say, "I wish I had a really nice suit like that. I bet I could get a job, if I had a really nice suit like that."

In truth the suit had been tailored just for the evangelist and had cost a pretty penny. Suddenly one of the shady characters hit the evangelist on the back of the head with a handgun. The three dragged him into the opening of an alley, stripped off his tailor-made suit, and with it got the thousands of dollars in cash he had meant to exchange for traveler's checks when he had the time.

this befallen you? and he replied, I have brought it all upon myself. Once I was journeying on the road and was making for the house of my father-in-law and I had with me three asses, one laden with food, one with drink and one with all kinds of dainties, when a poor man met me and stopped me on the road and said to me, Master, give me something to eat. I replied to him, Wait until I have unloaded something from the ass; I had hardly managed to unload something from the ass when the man died [from hunger]. I then went and laid myself on him and exclaimed, May my eyes which had no pity upon your eyes become blind, may my hands which had no pity on your hands be cut off, may my legs which had no pity upon your legs be amputated, and my mind was not at rest until I added, may my whole body be covered with boils. Thereupon his pupils exclaimed, 'Alas! that we see you in such a sore plight.' To this he replied, 'Woe would it be to me did you not see me in such a sore plight.'" (*b. Ta'anit* 21a [ca. sixth century C.E.]; from Epstein, 9.104-5)

There he was left, bleeding and naked. The pastor of the church where he had preached that morning passed by and saw a naked body lying in the alley, but could not see the body's face. Bemoaning the effect that drugs and alcohol have upon the lives of street people he resolved to write a column about it in the church newsletter the very next week.

A member of that same congregation passed by, quickening her steps and hiding the children's eyes from the man's nakedness. "Well, I never," she proclaimed, and the truth is, she hadn't.

Then along came an intern at Northwestern University Hospital from Baghdad, a Muslim. He had just come off three straight days on call and was dying to get some sleep. When he saw the man, though, he went to him, covered him with his own coat, stopped the bleeding, and called the ER he had just left to come get the man. The intern rode with him to the hospital, saw that he received the attention he needed, and arranged for the man to stay in the hospital until he was well.

"Now I ask you," the rabbi said to the religious scholar, "who was a neighbor to the evangelist who was robbed?"

"The one who helped him, I suppose."

"Then follow his example." There was just a hint of a smile on the rabbi's face as he turned away. *(Michael E. Williams)*

LUKE 11:1-13

The Friend at Midnight

A story about a persistent friend who makes a request at midnight provides a lesson on prayer and how God provides.

The Story

At one place after Jesus had been praying, one of his disciples said, 'Lord, teach us to pray, as John taught his disciples.' He answered, 'When you pray, say,

Father, may your name be
hallowed;
your kingdom come.
Give us each day our daily bread.
And forgive us our sins,
for we too forgive all who have done
us wrong.
And do not put us to the test.'

Then he said to them, 'Suppose one of you has a friend who comes to him in the middle of the night and says, "My friend, lend me three loaves, for a friend of mine on a journey has turned up at my house, and I have nothing to offer him"; and he replies from inside, "Do not bother me. The door is shut for the night; my children and I have gone to bed; and I cannot get up and give you what you want." I tell you that even if he will not get up and provide for him out of friendship, his very persistence will make the man get up and give him all he needs. So I say to you, ask, and you will receive; seek, and you will find; knock, and the door will be opened to you. For everyone who asks receives, those who seek find, and to those who knock, the door will be opened.

'Would any father among you offer his son a snake when he asks for a fish, or a scorpion when he asks for an egg? If you, bad as you are, know how to give good things to your children, how much more will the heavenly Father give the Holy Spirit to those who ask him!'

Comments on the Story

Although the parable proper is found in Luke 11:5-8, we must be aware of the larger context in order to interpret the Lukan use of the parable. The disciples are traveling with Jesus to Jerusalem. A disciple asks Jesus to teach them to pray. After all, John the Baptist had taught his disciples to pray. Prayer is a significant theme in Luke-Acts. Our passage tells the essence of Christian prayer and instructs the community how to pray.

My colleague J. Gerald Janzen has taught me that the prayer that Jesus teaches the disciples is a chiasm. Chiasm is a literary and rhetorical style in the ancient world in which the elements of a passage are divided into parallel members. The parallelism is from the outside members to the inner ones. As illustrated below, scholars usually identify the parallel members as A-A', B-B', etc. The centermost member(s) of the chiasm reveals its deepest concern. The members relate to one another in one of three types of parallelism: synonymous, in which the parallel elements say the same thing, but in other words; antithetical, in which the parallel elements contrast with each other; or synthetic, in which the parallel elements explain one another so that to understand one, the listener needs to hear it with the other. The prayer that Jesus taught the disciples is a synthetic chiasm.

A Father, may your name be hallowed;
B your kingdom come.
C Give us today our daily bread.
B' And forgive us our sins,
for we too forgive all who have done us wrong.
A' And do not put us to the test.

The disciples are to pray for God to manifest the divine rule (REB: kingdom). Whenever Jesus, the disciples, or the church pray in Luke and in Acts, an aspect of God's rule is revealed. The central petition of the prayer is for God to provide daily bread while the community is awaiting the complete demonstration of God's rule.

Bread is a significant symbol in Judaism. It represents that which is essential for life (Isaiah 58:7; Psalm 132:15; Ecclesiasticus 29:21). The reference to daily bread recalls God's daily provision of manna in the wilderness (Exodus 16:4-30; Psalm 78:20, 25). Some Jewish writers expected that, when the old age is ending and God's new age is beginning, God will provide a second supply of manna (*2 Baruch* 29:8; *Sibylline Oracles* 7:149; Revelation 2:17). Many Jewish theologians looked forward to a great banquet (presumably including bread) that would celebrate the end of evil and the complete manifestation of the divine rule (Isaiah 25:6-8). When the disciples and the church pray, they open themselves to receive the bread that God provides now and will provide even more abundantly in the future.

Jesus evokes these associations with bread in the parable proper. Jesus

> The rabbis also contrasted God's response to persistence with human responses. "R. Ze'era said: Suppose a man has a friend who so importunes him with his needs and his wants that the man comes to dislike him and tries to avoid him. But with the Holy One, blessed be He, it is not so. The more a man importunes God with his needs and his wants, the more God loves him." (*Midrash on Psalms* 4:3 [ca. ninth century C.E.]; from Braude, *Psalms,* 1.65-66)

begins the parable by engaging the listeners to think for themselves about how to interpret and apply the parable: "Suppose one of you. . . ." The listeners are invited to imagine themselves as the neighbor who is asleep at midnight.

In the ancient Near East, the rules of hospitality called for a host or hostess to provide a meal when a traveler arrived. Because of the dangers of being on the road at night (robbers, wild animals), travelers tried very hard to arrive at their destination by sundown. However, for an unexplained reason, the traveler in the parable does not arrive until midnight. Nonetheless, the family who furnishes lodging is obliged to provide a meal.

Not surprisingly, the midnight cupboard is bare. Cooks in those days often baked just enough bread for one day. Wanting to be hospitable, the householder goes to the neighbor's house, knocks on the door, and explains the need for bread. The neighbor is initially resistant. The children are asleep (and the listener is invited to remember how hard it can be to get children to drift into sleep). The door is locked with a cumbersome and noisy bar. The neighbor, likely tired, does not want to get up. However, the friend from next door is persistent. I can hear repeated knocking. To get rid of the noise, the neighbor finally provides the bread that is needed for the meal.

The parable is not an allegory in which the church is knocking and God is the recalcitrant neighbor. That would paint God in a terrible light. Quite the contrary, as the succeeding context reveals, the parable is an example (typical among the rabbis) of arguing from the lesser to the greater. If a cranky neighbor will arise and provide bread in the middle of the night to get rid of the knocking, *how much more* will God (whose generous character is revealed in Luke 6:27-38; 12:22-34) provide for the church.

A parent would not give a child a snake (an animal that is associated with the deception of Genesis 3:1-7) when the child asks for a fish (a sign of provision, Luke 9:10-17). Nor would a parent give a child a scorpion (a dangerous creature) when the child requests an egg (a source of nourishment).

If we evil parents know how to do good for our children, how much more will God "give the Holy Spirit to those who ask." The Holy Spirit is the agent through whom God continues the ministry of Jesus in the world. The Spirit empowers the church to witness to the coming of God's rule. In particular, the Spirit leads the church into the Gentile mission (Acts 2:14-21; 10:1–11:18) and sustains the church when it encounters difficulty.

To pray for bread is to turn to God for provision, both physical and spiritual, during the turning of the ages from old to new. In the Gospel of Luke, Jesus predicts that the disciples and the church will experience difficulty when they witness to the divine rule (Luke 12:4-12, 49-59; 21:12-19). In the book of Acts, Jesus' predictions come true as the church suffers for its witness.

In Acts, the church encounters resistance from both Jewish and Gentile peoples (Acts 4:1-22; 5:17-42; 6:8–8:1; 12:1-4; 13:48-51; 16:16-40; 17:1-15;

19:23-41; 21:27-36; 22:30–26:32; 27:13-44). However, God provides for the church. The community holds all its possessions in common so that there are no Christian needy (Acts 2:43-47; 4:32-37; 6:1-6). The disciples work miracles through the power of the Spirit (Acts 3:1-10; 5:12-16) and the Spirit leads the disciples into courageous testimony (Acts 3:11–4:22; 7:2-60). The Holy Spirit charges the church with the ecstatic awareness of the divine presence, power, and purposes (Acts 2:1-4; 10:44-48). In an act reminiscent of the exodus, the Holy Spirit opens prison doors (Acts 5:17-21; 12:6-11; 16:23-29).

This teaching on prayer is not a generic license for the followers of Jesus to ask for any old thing in the confidence that God will grant the request. The church is specifically enjoined to pray for the coming of the divine rule and for the courage to witness to that rule. By praying for daily bread, the Christian community turns to God for provision as the church waits for that rule and witnesses to it. The book of Acts assures the church that God does, indeed, provide.

In an unmistakable link to the parable, Luke describes the Lord's Supper as the breaking of bread (Luke 24:28-35; Acts 2:42; 20:7). The sacred meal is a means whereby God provides manna in the church's wilderness. The broken loaf is a sign of Christ's continuing presence in the church, and of the continuing trustworthiness of Christ's promise to return. Indeed, the Lord's Supper is a prefiguring of the great banquet that will take place after the second coming, which will function to celebrate the end of the evil of the old age and the beginning of the divine renewal of the world.

The parable is both a call and an encouragement. It calls us, as listeners, to pray for the coming of God's dominion and to witness to it. To pray is intentionally to open ourselves to the divine coming. The larger setting of Luke-Acts reminds us that such a witness may meet resistance. Just as God furnished manna for Israel in the wilderness and sustained the church in the book of Acts, so God provides bread for us. If I, as a parent, wrap my arms around my sobbing child and bind up her wounds, how much more will God do for the world.

Retelling the Story

> "If you, bad as you are, know how to give good things to your children, how much more will the heavenly Father give the Holy Spirit to those who ask him!" (Luke 11:13)

I had just fallen asleep, or it seemed that way, when the knock came on the door. At first I thought I was dreaming, then I heard the insistent pounding again. I looked at the travel alarm clock that sat next to the sleeper sofa where I was sleeping. It was one-thirty in the morning. I was home from seminary on a break and was assigned to bed down at night in the living room that my parents had added to the trailer in which I had grown up.

I slipped out of bed as quietly as I could and slowly pulled back the curtains that covered the front windows. A pretty beat-up version of an older model car was parked at the road. Why hadn't they pulled up into the gravel drive? I was afraid to walk to the door and move the small curtains that fit into the diagonal panes of glass that would have allowed me to see who was knocking.

For a long time I waited, hoping the visitor would tire of knocking or give up on the idea of waking anyone in the house. Finally the knocking stopped. Just as I turned to go back to bed, relieved that I would not have to deal with this particular problem tonight, the pounding came again, louder and more insistent this time. This guy was just not going to give up.

Every time the knocking came again my throat and stomach tightened, and I stopped breathing for a long moment. I was afraid. What if this guy was there to rob us, or worse, murder the entire family? I had read Truman Capote's *In Cold Blood* for a college class a couple of years earlier, and scenes from the book began to replay in my imagination. What if there was more than one stranger at the door? The truth of the matter is that I was not just scared—I was terrified.

I wasn't about to open the door to a stranger. What was I going to do? Though it made me feel more like the teenager I had been when I left home than the twenty-something man I was now, I went to wake my father. I touched his shoulder and spoke. "Daddy," I said. I hadn't called my father that for years. Finally, he awakened, and I told him that someone was at the door. He pulled on his clothes, walked through the living room, and opened the door. Through the storm door, which remained locked, I could see a thin man in work clothes. The stranger appeared to be in his fifties.

"What are you doing out at this hour?" I heard my father ask the visitor.

"Can I use your phone?" the stranger asked. His speech was slurred.

"It's late, and you've already woke up my son." For the first time irritation entered my father's voice.

"I just want to call my brother to come get my car started. I can't get it started." The man listed to one side, then the other.

After a brief hesitation my father reached for the latch on the storm door and opened it so the stranger could come in. I stood back, but I could still smell the alcohol on his breath. If our guest wasn't drunk, he was well on his way. My father showed the visitor to the small kitchen that had been part of the original trailer and turned on the light.

"There's the phone," my father told him. "Help yourself." Then he added, "You want some coffee?"

"That would be nice." The stranger sounded genuinely grateful. He dialed the number after two false starts, and I could hear him speaking into the telephone. At one point he turned and asked my father the address of our house. My father told him the number, then added, "Tell him it's about half a mile down from McWater's store."

After our visitor finished his call, he and my father sat at the table, talked, and drank coffee. As they talked they discovered that they knew many of the same people. I sat in the living room, read a book, and kept an eye on the kitchen until his brother came to retrieve our visitor.

When our visiting stranger and his brother were gone I asked my father why he had let the man in the house. Couldn't he tell that the fellow was drunk?

"His car wouldn't start. He needed to use the phone," was all he said.

"He could have come in here and killed us all, you know." I tried to make it sound as ominous as I could.

"I don't think so. I thought I knew him from the plant. His brother too; I think he works there too." My father sounded more tired than worried.

"His brother might have been in on it." I wasn't going to let it go.

"Well," my father turned to go back to bed, "you're the one studying to be a preacher. What do you think Jesus would have done?"

"He certainly wouldn't have let somebody in who could have killed him." My voice sounded angrier than I intended.

"He did though, didn't he?" My father's voice faded as he walked down the hallway toward his bedroom. *(Michael E. Williams)*

The Lost Coin

God is similar to a woman who searches for a lost coin and rejoices when she finds it.

The Story

Or again, if a woman has ten silver coins and loses one of them, does she not light the lamp, sweep out the house, and look in every corner till she finds it? And when she does, she calls her friends and neighbours together, and says, "Rejoice with me! I have found the coin that I lost." In the same way, I tell you, there is joy among the angels of God over one sinner who repents.'

Comments on the Story

The literary setting of this parable is important. Jesus is derided for eating with tax collectors and sinners (Luke 15:1-2). Tax collectors and sinners have abandoned God's ways and are disapproved of by the faithful. As my comments on tax collectors in connection with the parable of the Pharisee and the tax collector note (Luke 18:9-14), tax collectors were especially despised in Palestine. And in the first century, the term "sinner" was used to speak of persons who flagrantly disobeyed God. Eating together was a significant expression of hospitality in the ancient Near East.

The Pharisees and scribes "murmur" their disapproval. Their behavior echoes the murmuring of Israel against God in the wilderness (Exodus 15:24; 16:2, 7-8; 17:3; Numbers 11:1; 14:2, 27, 36; 16:11; Deuteronomy 1:27). Luke thus portrays the Pharisees and scribes as ungrateful and disobedient.

Jesus responds to the criticisms of the Pharisees and the scribes with a catena of parables: the lost sheep (discussed above in connection with Matthew 18:10-14), the lost coin, the loving parent (Luke 15:11-32), and the dishonest steward (Luke 16:1-15).

Luke repeatedly develops scenes in which male and female characters are parallel, or in which men and women are discussed in parallel fashion (Luke 2:25-38; 8:40-56; Acts 2:17-19; 5:1-10; 18:24-28). Luke also emphasizes the presence and leadership of women in the life and ministry of Jesus and in the early church (Luke 1:26-56; 7:11-17, 36-50; 8:1-3; 10:38-42; 13:10-17; 18:1-8; 21:1-4; 24:1-10; Acts 9:32-43; 12:12-17; 16:11-15). On the basis of such passages, many scholars believe that Luke is particularly concerned to show that

From the rabbis, the treasure to be sought would most often be the Torah itself: "The matter may be compared to the case of a king who lost gold in his house or pearls. Is it not through a wick that is worth a penny that he finds it again? So let a parable not be despised in your view, for it is through the parable that a person can master the words of the Torah. You may know that it is so, for lo, Solomon through parables mastered the smallest details of the Torah. R. Phineas b. Yair commenced by citing this verse: 'If you seek it like silver [and search for it as for hidden treasures, then you will understand the fear of the Lord and find the knowledge of God]' [Prov. 1:4-5]: If you seek words of the Torah like hidden treasures, the Holy One, blessed be He, will not withhold your reward. The matter may be compared to the case of a person, who, if he should lose a penny or a pin in his house, will light any number of candles, any number of wicks, until he finds them. Now the matter yields an argument *a fortiori:* If to find these, which are useful only in the here and now of this world, a person will light any number of candles, any number of wicks, until he finds them, as to words of Torah, which concern the life of the world to come as much as this world, do you not have to search for them like treasures?" (*Midrash Rabbah on the Song of Songs* 1.9 [sixth to eighth centuries C.E.]; from Boring-Berger-Colpe, 223, no. 329)

the rule of God restores women to an egalitarian place in community (much like the relationship enjoyed by Adam and Eve prior to Genesis 3).

The parable of the lost coin is fundamental to this theme because it compares God to a woman. In so doing, Jesus draws on a motif from Jewish literature (Deuteronomy 32:18; Isaiah 42:14; 49:13-15; 66:7-9, 13; Hosea 11:1-4). Moreover, the sensitive listener remembers from Genesis 1:26-27 that both men and women bear the image of God. And the community—when it is at its best—reflects the divine image when it is similar to the woman in the parable, seeking for the lost.

The fact that the woman expends so much effort to find one lost drachma probably indicates that she is poor. A drachma was a silver coin that was probably worth about a denarius, the wages of a laborer for one day and barely enough to sustain a household for a day. The ten coins—wages for ten days—may be her total wealth. A wealthy woman would not likely expend such energy for such a small amount of money.

She lights a lamp because Palestinian houses in the first century were notoriously dim. One-room houses (which were quite common) typically had only one window, or none at all. The lamp is probably a typical household fixture—a small, round clay dish with a hole on one side for the wick and another hole in the middle for receiving the oil. Hearing about the lighting of the lamp, the listener is invited to remember Jesus' sayings of

8:16 and 11:33. God has lit a light for the world. The church is to join Israel in shining it. A part of God's light is clarified by the actions of the woman in this story.

The floor may be dirt or stone (or some combination thereof). The broom—probably a stick with some thin leaves or twigs tied to one end—is able to pick up the coin by penetrating the loose dirt or the cracks in the stone paving.

The woman searches every corner of the house until she finds the missing drachma. The listener feels the extent, care, and urgency of the search.

When she finds the coin, she invites her "friends and neighbours" to rejoice with her. The Greek expression for "friends and neighbours" is expressed in the feminine case, which makes it clear that these too are women. The lost is found. When I hear these words, I imaginatively join the celebration of the women.

Jesus then draws a lesson from the parable, explaining that the angels in heaven rejoice similarly over one sinner who repents. For Luke, repentance is a twofold action. Persons who repent turn away from the brokenness, injustice, violence, and disobedience of the old world and their collusion therewith. They turn toward God and the restoration of the world that is under way through Jesus. Those who do not repent will perish in the apocalyptic cataclysm (Luke 3:7-17; 5:32; 13:1-9; 24:47; Acts 2:38; 3:19; 5:31-32; 8:22; 11:18; 17:30; 20:21; 26:20). The point is utterly clear: all who repent are welcome in God's dominion. And they should be welcome in the church, as well. Repentance, for Luke, is not a "work" but is a response empowered by the awareness of God's presence.

These latter emphases are underscored by the woman's invitation ("Rejoice with me") and by the joy in heaven. Joy, too, is a typical Lukan feature. In the Gospel of Luke and the book of Acts, joy usually breaks forth when an aspect of the rule of God is manifest (Luke 1:14, 44, 47; 2:10; 6:23; 10:17-20; 14:14; Acts 5:41; 8:8, 39; 11:23; 13:52; 14:17; 15:3, 31; 16:34). Many Jewish writings anticipate joy in the presence of God (and throughout the cosmos) when God's rule comes to expression in all times and places. When the church welcomes repentant sinners, it prefigures a dimension of the coming rule of God. And its joy is the exultation of the end times, already pouring forth.

This parable has a threefold invitation to the listener. First, the ministry of Jesus in Luke provides a paradigm for the ministry of the church in Acts, and the ministry of the church in Acts provides a paradigm for the ministry of the church in Luke's world. The parable reminds the church of its commission to search for tax collectors and sinners and others whom they represent. As the themes of the Gospel of Luke unfold in the book of Acts, we learn that the church is particularly called to invite Gentiles into the community of the new age. The parable invites the church to join God in seeking the lost.

Second, the parable invites the professional religious folk of the world, whom the story encodes as Pharisees and scribes, to welcome repentant tax collectors and sinners and others of similar character, for the latter have already been welcomed to God's own table. The contrast between the murmuring of the Pharisees and scribes (15:1-2) and the joy of the woman and the angels (15:9-10) is stark. The listener wonders, "Which would I rather be, especially when I recollect God's anger kindled against the Israelites who murmured in the wilderness?"

Third, the parable is also an invitation to tax collectors and sinners and those who are similar. It reminds them that God is searching for them (through the witness of the church) with pathos, determination, and intensity that surpass what the woman manifests in the story. God takes the initiative. But the search is not complete until the lost repent. Indeed, according to this parable, to repent is to be found.

This story is not merely an illustration. The parable creates an experience of being found. The parable lets us feel the rejoicing in heaven that takes place when one of us repents. The listeners are empowered to seek, and to repent, by the energy of the narrative world.

Retelling the Story

> "In the same way, I tell you, there is joy among the angels of God over one sinner who repents." (Luke 15:10)

The Teacher told this story:

There was a woman I knew some years ago who married late in life. Her husband was about the same age and, like her, had never married. They loved each other as well as any two people I have ever seen. It wasn't the kind of "need" love that youngsters feel, wanting someone to make them feel good about themselves. Nor was it the selfish love that drives people together for what each can get from the other, material or otherwise. No, it was a love that started out with a kind of maturity that few marriages ever reach, even after many years.

Since neither the woman nor the man was wealthy, she did not receive a diamond ring at the wedding. Her husband had offered, but she declined, knowing that the money could be better spent on more necessary things as they began their life together. They gave each other matching gold bands, symbols of the love and respect they had for each other.

After the rings were exchanged at their wedding she never saw her husband take his off, even to bathe or wash his hands. Over the years the ring seemed to be as much a part of him as the finger it encircled. The wife only removed her ring when she was digging in the garden or washing the dishes. She kept it in her pocket or on the shelf above the sink. Then, as soon as she had finished whatever she was doing, she would put the ring right back on the third finger of her left hand.

Occasionally she would lose track of her ring for a few hours, since it sometimes got moved behind something on the shelf or fell out of the pocket of her work pants when she took them off. Occasionally she would find the ring in the washer or dryer if those pants had gone into the wash before she remembered to search her pockets and retrieve the ring. Whenever she would look at her finger and find that her ring was not there, she knew that there were only four or five places where it might be found.

One day after the woman had worked in the garden and in several flowerbeds, then had taken off her work pants and washed and dried them, she found that her ring was missing again. She searched the usual places where it might be found, but her ring was nowhere to be seen. "I've just overlooked it," she thought to herself. So she returned to the garden and to each of the flowerbeds. She looked again in the clothes washer and the dryer to be sure she hadn't missed the ring there. She searched the floor and the closet, then under the bed near where she had taken the pants off before washing them, in case the ring had fallen out of her pocket. She scoured the sink and the shelf above it, even taking the traps off the pipes under the sink in case it had fallen there. Nothing!

It took the woman several days of fretting and going back over the places she had already searched before she told her husband that the ring was lost. "You'll come across it somewhere," he told her. "Don't worry about it," he reassured her, "I'll buy you another one." "I don't want another one," she told him, "I want the one you gave me on our wedding day." Though he said he never thought of it that way, she wondered if he saw her as being careless with or having disregard for their marriage, since she had lost the ring.

Several years passed and the woman's ring never turned up. Then after some time her husband was offered a job in another city. They were going to have to leave the house in which they had lived since their marriage. In some small way this idea cheered the woman, since this was an opportunity to move all the furniture, clear out the closets, and perhaps find her lost wedding ring. When the last piece of furniture was on the moving van, and the closets and the floors vacuumed, there was still no sign of her ring. As their car pulled away from their former home on its way to another city, she gave up all hope of ever finding her wedding ring.

Several more years passed. One day when the woman was vacuuming she pushed the tip of the vacuum cleaner wand deeper into the crevice between the arm of one of their living room chairs and the seat on which the cushion ordinarily sat. She heard a loud rattle like a piece of gravel being pulled up the length of the wand and into the vacuum bag. How did a piece of gravel get in that chair, she asked herself. She finished vacuuming the living room and, as she took the vacuum bag out to throw it away, she looked to see the size of the piece of gravel that had been in that chair. As she searched through the lint packed into the bag her hand found something hard, but it was not a piece of gravel. It was a ring. She pulled her hand out of the bag. It was her ring! She had forgotten all about sitting down to take off her shoes before washing her pants. It must have fallen out of her pocket then. The ring had remained between the arm and the seat of that chair through the move.

The woman felt like calling all her friends and inviting them to a party. The ring that she lost, this precious gift from her husband, had been found! She thought she would never see it again, and it had been found. Before she called her husband to give him the good news, the woman put the ring on the third finger of her left hand and promised herself that she would never take it off again. And she never did. *(Michael E. Williams)*

The Loving Parent

God's love is compared to that of a parent who lovingly responds to a wayward child and to a resentful older sibling.

The Story

Again he said: 'There was once a man who had two sons; and the younger said to his father, "Father, give me my share of the property." So he divided his estate between them. A few days later the younger son turned the whole of his share into cash and left home for a distant country, where he squandered it in dissolute living. He had spent it all, when a severe famine fell upon that country and he began to be in need. So he went and attached himself to one of the local landowners, who sent him on to his farm to mind the pigs. He would have been glad to fill his belly with the pods that the pigs were eating, but no one gave him anything. Then he came to his senses: "How many of my father's hired servants have more food than they can eat," he said, "and here am I, starving to death! I will go at once to my father, and say to him, 'Father, I have sinned against God and against you; I am no longer fit to be called your son; treat me as one of your hired servants.'" So he set out for his father's house. But while he was still a long way off his father saw him, and his heart went out to him; he ran to meet him, flung his arms round him, and kissed him. The son said, "Father, I have sinned against God and against you; I am no longer fit to be called your son." But the father said to his servants, "Quick! Fetch a robe, the best we have, and put it on him; put a ring on his finger and sandals on his feet. Bring the fatted calf and kill it, and let us celebrate with a feast. For this son of mine was dead and has come back to life; he was lost and is found." And the festivities began.

'Now the elder son had been out on the farm; and on his way back, as he approached the house, he heard music and dancing. He called one of the servants and asked what it meant. The servant told him, "Your brother has come home, and your father has killed the fatted calf because he has him back safe and sound." But he was angry and refused to go in. His father came out and pleaded with him; but he retorted, "You know how I have slaved for you all these years; I never once disobeyed your orders; yet you never gave me so much as a kid, to celebrate with my friends. But now that this son of yours turns up, after running through your money with his women, you kill the fatted calf for him." "My boy," said the father, "you are always with me, and everything I have is yours. How could we fail to celebrate this happy day? Your brother here was dead and has come back to life; he was lost and has been found."'

Comments on the Story

This parable, one of the best known and loved in the Gospel tradition, is the third in succession directed to the Pharisees and the scribes in response to their criticism of Jesus' table fellowship with tax collectors and sinners. (On the setting, see the interpretation of the parable of the lost coin above, Luke 15:8-10.)

The parable of the loving parent develops themes that are similar to the preceding parables, albeit with much greater narrative fullness. The passage vindicates Jesus' relationship with tax collectors and sinners. It encourages the church to welcome persons who are similar to the tax collectors and sinners in its time. It invites tax collectors and sinners to receive the welcome of God and the Christian community. A new element appears: this parable puts a significant question to the Pharisees and the scribes (and to those who are similar to them in later years, both inside the church and out). Will they join God's celebration of the return of the prodigals, or will they stand resentfully outside the house? As in the previous parables, the listener experiences this story in the hearing.

As the story begins, the younger offspring requests that offspring's share of the parent's estate. According to Near Eastern custom, this child's behavior is possible, but unusual. (For inheritance policies, see Numbers 27:8-11; 36:7-9; Deuteronomy 21:15-17; for advice against dispersing the estate before the parent's death, see Ecclesiasticus 33:19-23.) Because the sibling is the younger of two, the child would receive significantly less than the older one.

The philosopher Quintillian told a similar story. "Children are obligated to support their impoverished parents, or they deserve to be imprisoned. There was once a man who had two sons. The one was a good manager, the other a spendthrift. Both traveled into a far country and were captured by pirates. While they were captured, the spendthrift became sick. Both wrote home asking to be ransomed. The father immediately converted all his assets into cash and departed to redeem them. The pirates were not satisfied with the sum he had brought with him, saying that it hardly sufficed to ransom one son, and that he would have to make a choice. The father chose the sick son, who died soon after he had been released. Later, the other son managed to escape. Then, the impoverished father called on his son for support. The son refused. . . . [The father responded:] 'When a father of two sons redeems the sick one from the chains of slavery, this does not mean that he loves him more than the other. . . . So grant me support, because I wanted to redeem you, give me my bread, because I did redeem your brother." (Quintillian, *Declamatio* 5 [late first century C.E.]; from Boring-Berger-Colpe, 224, no. 331)

For the interpretation of the story, however, the most significant detail is this: by requesting the inheritance, the younger family member treats the parent as though the parent is dead. The Jewish listener is deeply disturbed, for this behavior violates the commandment to "honour your father and your mother . . ." (Exodus 20:12).

The child liquidates the inheritance, then travels to a distant country. The Jewish reader is further disturbed by the profligacy that results in the loss of the inheritance. Famine is sometimes a curse inflicted by God in consequence of disobedience of the covenant (Isaiah 51:19; Jeremiah 14:13-18; Amos 4:6). Such is the fate of those who leave the parent's house in violation of the community's sacred tradition.

The prodigal begins to work for a Gentile and to tend pigs. Swine, of course, are a traditional Jewish symbol of uncleanness (Leviticus 11:7; Deuteronomy 14:8). Indeed, not eating pork is a demonstration of fidelity (1 Maccabees 1:47; 2 Maccabees 6:18-19; 7:1). The mention of the swine evokes a visceral reaction in the hearer of the story. The prodigal is hungry enough to eat the long pods that the pigs eat.

> The rabbis also characterized a father's love for a wayward son in story form: "It is like a king's son who had gotten out of hand and was running wild, and the king sent his tutor after him and had him say: 'Search your conscience, feel remorse, my son!' But the son had the tutor say to his father, 'How can I face you, I am too ashamed.' Then his father sent these words to him, 'My son, should a son be ashamed to come back to his father? When you come home, are you not coming home to your father?'" (*Midrash Deuteronomy* 2:24 [ca. 800 C.E.]; from Boring-Berger-Colpe, 226, no. 334)

However, the errant heir comes to his senses. The Greek expression here is an idiom that also can mean "to repent" (as in *Testament of Joseph* 3:9). The young person remembers that the parent's hired servants have more food (and a better life), and resolves to confess the sin against God and family that has been manifest in the profligacy, in the hope of being received at least as a servant in the parent's house. Such an attitude is the essence of repentance. (On repentance, see the comments above on the parable of the lost coin, Luke 15:8-10.)

The most remarkable element of the story is the parent's reaction. The parent sees the refugee while the refugee is still a long way off. In a gesture that was highly uncharacteristic of a parent in Mediterranean antiquity, the parent *runs* to greet the returnee. The Greek for "heart went out" is the same term that is translated "moved to pity" in reference to Jesus when he encountered the widow at Nain (Luke 7:13) and in the story of the compassionate Samaritan (Luke 10:33). The parent *feels* the need of the offspring and responds accordingly.

The parent embraces and kisses the refugee (traditional signs of acceptance) before the latter speaks a single word. The parent's behavior is a model of grace itself.

The parent orders a robe (a signal of wealth and prestige), a signet ring so that the child can affix the family seal on important documents, and shoes (a mark of affluence). The repentant one is fully reinstated into the household with all rights and privileges thereunto (compare Genesis 45:14-15; 46:29). A celebration is instantly prepared utilizing the fatted calf, the most succulent of the herd. The first-century hearer recognizes echoes of the final banquet that celebrates the establishment of God's rule.

The younger child had become the same as a Gentile. In that state, the prodigal was lost. Indeed, to be lost in that way is to be dead. But now, the parent—whom the child regarded as dead at the opening of the parable—resurrects the young person.

In this part of the story, the first-century listener would recognize thematic similarities to the relationship between the Jewish and Gentile peoples. Though the Jewish people and the Gentiles are born of one parent, the Gentiles (figuratively speaking) have lived in a distant country among swine and have treated God as dead. Nonetheless, Jewish theologians anticipated the manifestation of the rule of God when the Gentiles would repent of their idolatry and swine-like life. The two peoples would be reunited in the family and service of the one living God (Isaiah 11:10; Tobit 14:4-7; 13:6; see also *1 Enoch* 10:21; 90:30, 38; 91:14). In fact, Israel and the church are ordained to shine God's light in the world for the benefit of the Gentiles (Genesis 12:1-3; Isaiah 49:1-7; Luke 2:32; 8:16-18; 11:33-36; Acts 13:47; 26:23).

Despite their long years of neglect, idolatry, and disobedience, the heart of the divine parent still responds with love to the Gentiles. Through Christ is expressed the divine love for those still in distant lands. As Luke makes clear in Acts 10:1–11:15, the same full blessing of the Spirit that has animated Judaism during its long life is now pouring out on repentant Gentiles as well.

The older heir is working on the farm and hears the sound of the music and dancing coming from the house. When told that the younger brother is being welcomed home with a party, the older one becomes angry and refuses to enter the house. The parent comes out of the house and pleads. This language prompts the listener to remember God's pleading with Israel in the First Testament to return to the covenantal life. For instance, we feel the pathos of the divine pleading in Hosea 2:1-15 (see also 11:1-12; Jeremiah 31:18-20) in the parent's pleading with the older child.

The elder sibling reminds the parent of the former's long and obedient service on the farm, "yet you never gave me so much as a kid, to celebrate with my friends." (A kid was not as impressive as the prize, fatted calf.) The parent replies, "You are always with me," language that is reminiscent of the divine promise of God to Israel, "I will be with you." The latter expression nearly always implies God's pledge to redeem Israel or to work for Israel's good (Exodus 3:12; Isaiah 43:2).

"All that is mine is yours," the parent says. None of the inheritance of the older offspring is taken away. Every promise is still in force. All that the parent asks is for the elder heir to acknowledge that the younger now has a place at the family table. As the story closes, the reluctant sibling is still standing outside the house. This latter person is in danger of being as lost in the backyard of the family home as the younger child was in the swine pens of the distant country.

The listener recollects that this parable was sparked by Jesus' defense of eating with tax collectors and sinners in the face of the charges of Pharisees and scribes (Luke 15:1-2). Jesus' table fellowship with tax collectors and sinners is a celebration of those who are returning to God, in much the same way that the banquet for the younger child celebrates the return to the family home. The situation of the older brother in the story is thus suggestive of the situation of the Pharisees and scribes. God is throwing a welcome party for sinners, while conventional religious leaders stand outside, grumble, and exclude themselves from the party.

Listeners wonder whether the older progeny will join the party or stay outside. This ending provokes the listener. "Will I join the celebration—and multiply the joy of the gathering (especially the parent)? Or will I stay out?"

While this parable is not an allegory, it implicitly compares the situation of the two siblings with that of the church and Judaism. The church's Gentile mission is a part of God's ingathering of the Gentiles in the last days. The church is called to be a community that welcomes Gentiles and celebrates their coming to God. The promises of God to the Jewish people are not revoked. The ministry of Jesus and the church do not call into question the status of the Jewish community (Luke 5:31). The question in the parable is whether the Jewish people take the elder child's attitude toward the Christian mission, or whether they will acknowledge the validity of that mission.

In Luke's context, the story had the quality of prophetic self-criticism similar to that found in Isaiah, Jeremiah, Hosea, and others of the prophets. Given the centuries of anti-Semitism since Luke, today's preacher, teacher, or storyteller must handle this theme with care so as not to reinforce negative stereotypes of the Jewish people. Many in today's Jewish community willingly acknowledge that the church is a community that is genuinely beloved of the God of Israel. Many Jewish leaders today seek opportunities for Judaism and Christianity to engage in mutual witness for the one living God. My observation is that the attitude of the elder sibling is frequently found today among church members who do not recognize the continuing validity of Judaism, or who refuse to acknowledge that God is welcoming persons and communities today who are as different from Christians as Gentiles were from Jewish people in the first century.

Retelling the Story

> "How could we fail to celebrate this happy day? Your brother here was dead and has come back to life; he was lost and has been found." (Luke 15:32)

Liz and her mother were having yet another argument. Mary, her mother, wanted Liz home too early. And Liz's friends? Too wild. Finally, Liz looked angrily at her mother and said, "I wish you were dead." She turned and walked out the front door.

Slam!

Mary put her head in her hands and covered her eyes so Greta, her other daughter, couldn't see her crying.

Greta put her hand on her mother's back and said, "Liz didn't mean what she said. You know that, Mom. She'll be back. She's done this before."

"Oh Greta, I know," said Mary. "But Liz is so much more independent and argumentative than you were. Her friends are the wrong type, no good for her."

Liz didn't come back that night. She didn't come back the next morning. Mary contacted Liz's friends and finally the police. Nothing. She was gone. She had disappeared. Days became weeks. Weeks became months. Months turned into a year. Then two years. Simply gone. Liz became one in the long list of missing persons whose pictures appeared in the newspaper. Was she even alive? What were the chances?

Then one day Mary received a call. "Mother, I'm so sorry. I'm so sorry." Tears welled up in Mary's eyes. "Can you forgive me? You were right about my friends. You know, sex and drugs. I thought I knew so much. I knew enough not to be afraid of hard drugs, not to be afraid to use sex for money. Now I have AIDS."

Mary listened silently and wept. Then she said, "Come home, Liz. I'll arrange airfare. Come home, I want to see you. I want to hold you again."

The next day Mary went to the airport and stood outside the gate waiting for Liz to walk through. Liz had changed; she was pale, and too thin. But Mary recognized her immediately, ran up, and embraced Liz when she appeared outside the security area. They rocked back and forth saying nothing. Simply weeping joyfully. Mary drove the old car home as Liz looked out the window. When they approached the old neighborhood, the trees were wrapped with yellow ribbons. And as they got closer, there were more and more yellow ribbons. "Oh, Mother, you didn't, did you?" asked Liz.

"In one day, no. I had help, Liz," said Mary. Cars lined the street outside Mary's house. Tables burgeoning with food crowded the front yard on this Sunday afternoon. Mary parked the old car. Friends and relatives crowded around the car.

"Oh, Mother, I'm so embarrassed," said Liz.

"Liz, the past is the past," Mary said. "I told everyone what happened. We are just happy you are with us again."

Liz climbed out of the car. One person after another embraced her. She talked with one person, then another, working her way around the front yard. Then Liz asked Mary, "Where's Greta? I haven't seen her."

Mary found Greta in her bedroom. "What's wrong, Greta?" asked Mary.

"Mother, it is so embarrassing to have Liz here," said Greta. "A prostitute and junkie for a sister? How can you have a party for her?"

"And not for you?" Mary asked.

"Yes, you love her more than me. I have never done anything like this. I've done everything a daughter should do. Yet you celebrate her faults."

"Oh, Greta, I thought Liz was dead. But she is alive. Do you know what that means to me? If you could possibly add up all the love we've shared these last years, it would be far, far more than Liz gets today. Besides, this is not Liz's party. When someone returns from the dead, the party is for all who come." *(Bruce J. Ackerson)*

From the rabbis: "*Return, O Israel, unto the Lord thy God.* Consider the parable of a prince who was far away from his father—a hundred days' journey away. His friends said to him: 'Return to your father.' He replied: 'I cannot: I have not the strength.' Thereupon his father sent word, saying to him: 'Come back as far as you can according to your strength, and I will go the rest of the way to meet you.' So the Holy One, blessed be He, says to Israel: *Return unto Me, and I will return unto you* (Mal. 3:7)." (*Pesiqta Rabbati* 44.9 [sixth to seventh centuries C.E.]; from Braude, *Pesikta rabbati,* 779)

LUKE 16:1-15

The Dishonest Steward

A dishonest steward, who cheats his employer, is a model of what the followers of Jesus are not to be like.

The Story

He said to his disciples, 'There was a rich man who had a steward, and he received complaints that this man was squandering the property. So he sent for him, and said, "What is this that I hear about you? Produce your accounts, for you cannot be steward any longer." The steward said to himself, "What am I to do now that my master is going to dismiss me from my post? I am not strong enough to dig, and I am too proud to beg. I know what I must do, to make sure that, when I am dismissed, there will be people who will take me into their homes." He summoned his master's debtors one by one. To the first he said, "How much do you owe my master?" He replied, "A hundred jars of olive oil." He said, "Here is your account. Sit down and make it fifty, and be quick about it." Then he said to another, "And you, how much do you owe?" He said, "A hundred measures of wheat," and was told, "Here is your account; make it eighty." And the master applauded the dishonest steward for acting so astutely. For in dealing with their own kind the children of this world are more astute than the children of light.

'So I say to you, use your worldly wealth to win friends for yourselves, so that when money is a thing of the past you may be received into an eternal home.

'Anyone who can be trusted in small matters can be trusted also in great; and anyone who is dishonest in small matters is dishonest also in great. If, then, you have not proved trustworthy with the wealth of this world, who will trust you with the wealth that is real? And if you have proved untrustworthy with what belongs to another, who will give you anything of your own?

'No slave can serve two masters; for either he will hate the first and love the second, or he will be devoted to the first and despise the second. You cannot serve God and Money.'

The Pharisees, who loved money, heard all this and scoffed at him. He said to them, 'You are the people who impress others with your righteousness; but God sees through you; for what is considered admirable in human eyes is detestable in the sight of God.'

Comments on the Story

The story of the dishonest manager is one of the most difficult parables to interpret. I will first recount some interpretive details on which virtually all scholars agree. I will then report the current scholarly consensus. Finally I will offer my own, admittedly idiosyncratic, interpretation.

Most scholars agree that the parable itself is found in Luke 16:1-8a. The sayings in verses 9-13 were appended to the parable by Luke in order to clarify its meaning.

A wealthy person has a steward. In this very common arrangement in antiquity, the steward was a manager who operated with a great deal of authority. While a steward could be a slave, many stewards in antiquity were (like the one in our story) free employees. In many instances, the word of the steward was the same as that of the owner. The steward could manage the household and its servants and properties, direct farming and manufacturing operations, and lease, buy, and sell. The steward handled the owner's money and was empowered to lend it with interest.

The wealthy person receives a report that the steward is squandering the money. He calls the steward to give an account, and dismisses the employee. Through a soliloquy, we have access to the steward's clever reasoning: not strong enough to dig, too proud to beg, he will use the economic power still available through the office of steward to create advantageous relationships with business partners that will continue beyond the dismissal. The steward "buys" friends.

An ancient Egyptian maxim presents a similar sentiment to that of this parable: "Take care to use what has been apportioned to you to keep your close friends happy, as one who has been rewarded by God. There is no one who knows well his plans, who only thinks as far ahead as tomorrow. When another occasion of reward comes, then the people come to him and say 'Welcome.'" (*Instruction of the Vizier Ptah-hotep* [ca. tenth century B.C.E.]; from Boring-Berger-Colpe, 226, no. 335)

The steward reduces the amount that major debtors owe the owner. A debt of a hundred jars of olive oil is reduced to fifty. A debt of a hundred measures of wheat is reduced to eighty. Some commentators contend that the discount is simply the steward's commission. However, if this were the case, the steward would not be in serious trouble with the owner. The steward does not deny the inference of wrongdoing. The steward cheats the wealthy person one last time.

Surprisingly, the owner applauds the manager's astuteness. Is Jesus holding up the behavior of the steward as a paradigm for the community? According to the most widespread scholarly interpretation, the steward is not a *direct* model whose unethical behavior is to be emulated. Luke does not commend illegality. Rather, in the freedom of the storyteller, Luke uses the manager's prudence in a situation of extremity as a way to encourage the church to realize that it needs to be as creative in its witness to the rule of God. The church is not to violate its own tradition, but it is to be as clever as the steward. In this view, the story is a subtle argument from the lesser to the greater: if the manager could be so shrewd in temporal affairs, how much more imaginative the church should be in the affairs of the divine rule.

In my opinion, the Lukan context, and other details within the parable and in the sayings in verses 9-13, argue for another interpretation. In Luke 15:1-2, the Pharisees and the scribes murmur against Jesus' table companionship with tax collectors and sinners, much like the people of Israel murmured against Moses in the wilderness. As listeners, we are predisposed against the Pharisees and the scribes. Jesus speaks to them to defend table fellowship with tax collectors and sinners by means of the parables of the lost sheep (15:3-7), the lost coin (15:8-10), and the loving parent (15:11-32). The first two parables create images of the divine search for those who are lost. Lost sheep and lost coins can be found through repentance.

The first part of the parable of the loving parent illustrates someone who becomes lost, but then is found through repentance. The second part of the same parable implicitly compares the situation of the Pharisees and the scribes to that of the elder sibling. They refuse to join the celebration that is Jesus' table fellowship with tax collectors and sinners. Even worse, they murmur against it. This catena of parables moves from God's search for, and welcome of, the lost tax collectors and sinners to the Pharisees, who are lost by virtue of their unwillingness to acknowledge the validity of the mission to the tax collectors, sinners, and Gentiles.

From this perspective, Jesus tells the parable of the dishonest manager (and the subsequent sayings) to the disciples in order to reveal the dissolute character of the Pharisees. The behavior of the manager is reprehensible. Indeed, the Greek word for "squandering" is the same one that describes the behavior of the profligate younger child in Luke 15:13. The occurrence of this expression in the parable of the dishonest steward suggests that the steward is in much the same moral situation as the younger sibling in the preceding story. The steward's behavior violates the community's tradition regarding the use of money and the practice of justice in the community. This picture of the Pharisees is consistent with Luke 11:37-54.

The contrast between the younger child (Luke 15:11-32) and the manager is striking. In the pigsty, the prodigal repents and is restored to the family home. The owner discovers that the manager is pilfering the household bank and confronts the manager. Instead of repenting, the steward runs a further scam in the hope of "buying" places to stay after being dismissed. According to 16:14-15, the Pharisees overhear Jesus' remarks and scoff at them. Luke describes the Pharisees as lovers of money. This narrative setting thus gives Jesus the opportunity to render a decisive negative judgment on the Pharisees (v. 15).

The Pharisees impress others with behavior that appears to be righteous. In particular, they avoid contact with tax collectors and sinners. But God sees through the Pharisees (literally, "God knows your hearts"). The heart is the center of the self, the point at which thought, feeling, and will coalesce: "Where your treasure is, there will your heart be also" (Luke 12:34; cf. Luke 6:45). According to Jesus, the way to true "wealth" is through selling possessions and giving alms, for these actions create "never-failing treasure in heaven" (12:33). In the parable of the barn builder (Luke 12:13-21), wealth is to be used for building up all in the community. True security (treasure in heaven) comes by putting one's wealth at the service of the community (Acts 2:43-47; 4:32-35). By scheming for self-centered preservation, the dishonest manager—and the Pharisees—subvert the very possibilities that might lead to the true security that results from communal sharing. (On the Pharisees' love of wealth and distorted priorities, see further Luke 11:37-54, esp. 42-44.)

In this view, verse 9 is ironic ("use your worldly wealth to win friends for yourselves"). The use of wealth that is characteristic of the Pharisees (see v. 15) does not win real friends. Nor does it create a place in the eternal home. According to Luke 16:10-12, the misuse of wealth (characteristic of the Pharisees) is a "small matter" of untrustworthiness that points to the failure of the Pharisees to be trustworthy in larger matters, especially with "the wealth that is real," that is, with things pertaining to the divine rule. While the Pharisees want both to serve God and to have money, they cannot (16:13). The Pharisees currently love money and human recognition more than they love God (16:14). The parables of Luke 15:1–16:15 invite them to repent.

As indicated in the introductory section, "Reading the Parables," the preacher, teacher, and storyteller need to handle such criticism of the Pharisees with care, especially given the contribution of this type of thinking to anti-Semitism. We should note that the behavior imputed to the Pharisees here is today all too often exhibited by church members themselves. But, as Luke 15:32 says, such individuals can repent of their love of human recognition and money and join the celebration.

Retelling the Story

"You cannot serve God and Money." (Luke 16:13c)

Oh uncle, my uncle, you are the wealthiest man in town. Who has a nicer home? Who wears finer clothes? Who drives a larger car? Who eats better than you? God blesses you in every way.

Oh uncle, my uncle, they call you God's servant. You attend church every Sunday. And help those whom you know. You strive to have God's word in all the schools. Surely you fear and praise God.

Oh uncle, my uncle, you stand for freedom and democracy and personal responsibility. Proudly you command God to bless America.

Oh uncle, my uncle, why then won't you deal with the scoundrel? He beats his wife and enslaves his family. He threatens his neighbors. Why do you say nothing?

Oh uncle, my uncle, must you buy such friends? Does he threaten your easy life? Are you too weak to dig or too proud to beg? Is your easy life worth more than his family's freedom? Under what rock is your anger hidden?

Oh uncle, my uncle, when do you venture outside your gated neighborhood? When do you see the misery of the poor and the hungry? AIDS spreads like wildfire through their homes.

Oh uncle, my uncle, you welcome God's wrath to punish their sexual promiscuity. When will you look into the large, sad eyes of the orphaned child? Is she responsible? Why does God punish her?

Oh uncle, my uncle, will you not see the mother weeping for the sick, hungry boy? Can you spare one thin dime? Gladly will they eat the crumbs from your overflowing table or your waste tipped into the trash.

Oh uncle, my uncle, your love of money betrays God's blessing. If you prove untrustworthy with the wealth of this world, who will trust you with the wealth that is real?

Oh uncle, my Uncle Sam, whatever will we do with you? *(Bruce J. Ackerson)*

The Rich Person and Lazarus

A rich person feasts in this life and ignores the needs of poor, hungry Lazarus, but in the next world their fates are reversed.

The Story

There was once a rich man, who used to dress in purple and the finest linen, and feasted sumptuously every day. At his gate lay a poor man named Lazarus, who was covered with sores. He would have been glad to satisfy his hunger with the scraps from the rich man's table. Dogs used to come and lick his sores. One day the poor man died and was carried away by the angels to be with Abraham. The rich man also died and was buried. In Hades, where he was in torment, he looked up and there, far away, was Abraham with Lazarus close beside him. "Abraham, my father," he called out, "take pity on me! Send Lazarus to dip the tip of his finger in water, to cool my tongue, for I am in agony in this fire." But Abraham said, "My child, remember that the good things fell to you in your lifetime, and the bad to Lazarus. Now he has his consolation here and it is you who are in agony. But that is not all: there is a great gulf fixed between us; no one can cross it from our side to reach you, and none may pass from your side to us." "Then, father," he replied, "will you send him to my father's house, where I have five brothers, to warn them, so that they may not come to this place of torment?" But Abraham said, "They have Moses and the prophets; let them listen to them." "No, father Abraham," he replied, "but if someone from the dead visits them, they will repent." Abraham answered, "If they do not listen to Moses and the prophets they will pay no heed even if someone should rise from the dead."'

Comments on the Story

In 15:1-2, the Pharisees and scribes murmur against Jesus' table fellowship with tax collectors and sinners. I discussed the cumulative effect of the setting of Luke 15:1–16:15 in connection with the parable of the dishonest steward (Luke 16:1-15). That section concludes with a combination of heavy criticism of the Pharisees and pastoral warning to the Christian community to be faithful in both small and great matters. Luke 16:16-18 segues into the parable of the rich person and Lazarus by reminding the listener that the provisions of the law and the prophets are still in force to provide guidance in how to be faithful. The dishonest steward would not have been dismissed if the steward had followed their prescriptions. The Pharisees and the scribes would not murmur if they took to heart the best of their own tradition.

The parable of the rich person and Lazarus raises the stakes in Luke's critique of the Pharisees and in his pastoral warning to the church. The parable calls the Christian community to practice the justice advocated by the law and the prophets, or face the consequences meted out to the rich person.

The rich person lives in extraordinary opulence. The color purple was associated with those who lived at the upper echelons of economic and social power in antiquity. In most households, feasting was reserved for special occasions; the rich person feasts sumptuously every day. These details impress the hearer with the magnitude of this person's wealth. The listener also thinks of fine dress in connection with the scribes (Luke 20:45-47) and, by association, with their comrades the Pharisees.

Listeners are empathetic when Luke describes Lazarus as poor and covered with sores (ulcers), languishing by the rich person's gate day after day. One can feel the ulcerations oozing. The emotional effect of this description is intensified by adding that the dogs lick the sores. To ancient people, to be licked by a dog in such a way would be a sign of utter humiliation.

The name Lazarus means "one whom God helps." The meaning of the name indicates the only source of help for Lazarus. Despite the fact that the impoverished and ulcerated Lazarus lay at the rich person's gate, the wealthy one paid no attention.

Lazarus dies. According to Jewish thinking, each human being is entitled to respectable burial. However, Lazarus

Jesus' parable seems to echo this popular contemporary Egyptian story found on a first-century papyrus fragment: "[Once] it happened that Setme heard [loud funeral] lamentations. [He] looked from [the balcony of] his house [and saw a rich man,] who was being carried to his grave with [loud] cries of lamentation, with much pomp [and richly decorated funeral accessories]. He looked [again, and there he saw] below him a poor man from Memphis being carried to the graveyard, wrapped in a mat . . . , without [anyone at all] following it. [Then said] Setme: 'By [Ptah, the great god, how much better off are the rich,] who are buried amidst great lamentation and with great honor, than the poor, who are taken to the graveyard without an escort.' [Then said Si-osire: 'May it go with you in the realm of the dead, as it will happen to this poor man in the realm of the dead [and not as it will happen to this rich man] in the place [of judgment.] You will [perceive that, when you] come into the realm of the dead.' [Si-osire leads Setme through the realm of the dead. . . .] Then Setme saw an elegant, prominent man, clothed in a garment of fine linen, near the is denied even this minimal dignity, and must be carried to be "close beside" Abraham (Greek: "in the bosom of Abraham") by the angels. "The bosom of Abraham" is a figure of speech that indicates a position of honor at the banquet of the afterlife (see the third "parallel story" attached to this chapter).

Upon death, the rich person is buried, but burial is the last of life's amenities, for the wealthy person awakes in Hades and finds himself in a place of fiery torment. While Jewish understandings of Hades varied in the first century C.E., Luke presumes that it is much like the blazing pit of so many popular descriptions today. Hades (sometimes known by the designations hell, Gehenna, or the place of weeping and wailing and gnashing of teeth) is specifically for the punishment of the wicked. One can feel the unremitting heat and the wealthy person's parched tongue.

The rich person pleads with Abraham for pity. The one now dressed in smoldering purple rags wants Lazarus to bring some water. He who showed no mercy toward Lazarus in this life now begs for mercy from God. One can feel desperation in the plea of the wealthy person. We also learn that he knew Lazarus in their former life, for he calls Lazarus by name. This recognition adds to the sadness of the rich person's prior neglect. We are also reminded that the person of means is never named in this parable. God (and the listener) knows Lazarus by name. But the identity of the rich person is lost, as is the temporal opulence of the purple, the fine linen, and the sumptuous daily feasts.

place where Osiris [the lord of the underworld] was seated . . . That is the poor man from Memphis you saw being carried to the graveyard, wrapped in a mat, without a funeral procession. . . . His good deeds [on earth] were found more numerous than his sins, and . . . it was commanded before Osiris that the rich funeral vestments of the rich man you saw being carried out with much honor and praise be given to the aforementioned poor man, and that he be given a place among the elevated transfigured ones as a man of god who serves Sokaris-Osiris, near the residence of Osiris.

This rich man whom you saw was brought into the underworld, and his sins were balanced against his good deeds. His sins were found to be more numerous than the good deeds he had done on the earth; it was commanded that recompense be made in the underworld. [He is the man] from whom you have seen how the hinge-pin of the gate to the realm of the dead has been left in his right eye . . . while his mouth is open in loud lamentations. . . . Whoever is good on earth, to that person the underworld is also good, and to whomever is evil on earth, it goes badly [there]." (from Boring-Berger-Colpe, 227-28, no. 338)

Abraham replies that the fortunes of the wealthy and the poor are now permanently reversed. The hearer recollects the beatitudes in Luke 6:20-21 and the woes in 6:24-25. Furthermore, the place of Abraham's bosom and the place of torment are separated by a great, uncrossable chasm. The wealthy person's daily decision (or nondecision) to neglect the ulcerated Lazarus at the gate has consequences that are eternal and irremediable.

The rabbis also told a version of this story: "There were two holy men. . . . One of them died, and he was not properly mourned. But when . . . the village tax collector died, the whole town took time off to mourn him. The surviving holy man began to weep saying, 'Woe, for [the enemies] of Israel will have nothing.' [The deceased holy man] appeared to him in a dream, and said to him, 'Do not despise the sons of your Lord. This one did one sin, and the other one did one good deed, and it went well for [the latter on earth, so while on earth I was punished for my one sin, he was rewarded for his one good deed].' Now what was the culpable act which the holy man had done? . . . He committed no culpable act in his entire life. But one time he put on the phylactery of the head before that of the hand. Now what was the meritorious deed which . . . the village tax collector had done? . . . He never did a meritorious deed in his life. But one time he made a banquet for the councilors of his town but they did not come. He said, 'Let the poor come and eat the food, so that it not go to waste.' There are, moreover, those who say that he was traveling along the road with a loaf

The suffering wealthy person has five siblings who are still in the family house and who evidently enjoy a lush lifestyle just as he had. They also apparently demonstrate the same neglect for the poor. The rich person requests the patriarch to send a messenger to warn the family so that they can change their attitudes and behavior (that is, repent) and avoid the torment of Hades. This concern is the first that the rich person shows for others in the parable—and it is restricted to his own family.

Abraham replies that the writings of Moses and the prophets provide sufficient guidance for how the wealthy are to live in community with the poor. Indeed, these materials are permeated with forceful instructions to provide for the poor of the land (Exodus 22:21-22; Leviticus 19:9-10; Deuteronomy 10:17-19; 15:1-11; Isaiah 58:3; Jeremiah 5:25-29; Hosea 12:7-9; Amos 2:6-8; Micah 3:1-3). The listener thinks of passages such as Amos 6:4-7, in which the feasting of the wealthy, who do not practice justice for the poor, is a sign of their disobedience and a part of the reason for the downfall of the nation.

At this juncture, incidentally, we can see clearly that for Luke, Jesus and the

Christian mission do not supersede Judaism. To be sure, Luke polemicizes against certain Jewish people and practices, but Luke does not reject Judaism as such. The church extends and adapts the essence of Judaism for the sake of the Gentile members of the Christian community. This parable, and other teachings of Luke, emphasize that the care of the poor is an essential expression of Jewish and Christian identity.

of bread under his arm, and it fell. A poor man went and picked it up, and the tax collector said nothing to him so as not to embarrass him. After a few days the holy man saw his fellow [in a dream] walking among gardens, orchards, and fountains of water. He saw . . . the village tax collector with his tongue hanging out by a river. He wanted to reach the river but he could not reach it." (*p. Sanhedrin* 6:23c, 30-43 [fifth century C.E.]; from Boring-Berger-Colpe, 228-29, no. 338)

The rich person counters that the family will repent if they are visited by someone from the dead. The mention of repentance impresses the listener with the fact that repentance, in Luke, is more than a change of heart; true repentance results in the use of one's material resources for God's purposes, particularly for the upbuilding of a just community that mediates divine provision, especially for the poor.

At the climax of the parable, Abraham responds that those who do not listen to Moses and the prophets will not listen, "even if someone should rise from the dead." The listener, of course, knows that Jesus has risen from the dead. Yet many who are similar to the rich person (and to the Pharisees and scribes in the larger context of the parable) do not repent. The parable explains why the news of the resurrection does not bring about a change of heart and behavior among such individuals. They serve Money, and other idols, rather than the God whose will is revealed in the law and the prophets.

As we hear the parable, we contrast the self-centered feasts of the wealthy person with the banquet given by the loving father to celebrate the return of the prodigal in Luke 15:11-32. The former results in an afterlife in the torment of Hades. Repentance could result in a place at the eternal banquet given by the great parent of the universe.

The listener also contrasts the behavior of the rich person and the Pharisees with that of Jesus. The former eat only with members of the household. Jesus eats with tax collectors and sinners. The former celebrate a feast leading to death. The latter is the meal that leads to life. While Lazarus does not bear the moral onus of the tax collectors and sinners, he, like them, is an outcast. The parable thus encourages us to use our tables as means of grace.

The listener further recollects the common meals of the early church and the nascent Christian community's provision for all through the sharing of possessions. The contrast is stark between the rich person who will not even give

Lazarus the scraps from the table, and the early church, which "held everything in common," "distributed to everyone according to his need," and "shared their meals with unaffected joy" (Acts 2:44-47).

The parable faces the listener with stark questions. With whom do I want to identify now and in the age to come? What actions do I need to take in order to enact the teaching of Moses and the prophets to provide for the poor? *We* still have time to repent.

Retelling the Story

> "If they do not listen to Moses and the prophets they will pay no heed even if someone should rise from the dead." (Luke 16:31)

Lazarus slid along the white stone into the sunlight, rubbing his hands as he went. "Brrr," he said. "No gloves. I sure wish I had some gloves." The wall glistened against the clear blue sky. He squinted as he looked out at the black asphalt parking lot. Shiny new cars and SUVs lined up in neat rows. Lazarus tipped his head back against the wall as the muffled sound of singing broke through the silence of the morning. Then the carillon sounded the end of the service. Lazarus placed his hat at the end of the stump where his right leg used to be. He winced and rubbed his stomach.

The parishioners exited the Sunday worship looking happy and self-satisfied. They walked past Lazarus in their Sunday best, caught up in conversation, slipping on gloves, and adjusting outerwear. One man briefly looked at Lazarus and then looked away. A little girl pulled on her mother's arm and looked distressed to see Lazarus in such a condition. "Don't worry," said the mother, "our church helps these people. Hurry up now, we'll be late for brunch." A small boy pointed to the beggar. His father muttered, "He's an alcoholic. If we give him money, he'll only get drunk." Another whispered to her friend, "He's mentally ill. That's why he's homeless." And another said, "Did he cough? Be careful, he probably has that incurable form of TB." A man said to his teenager, "I don't mind helping the poor. I just don't want to see them." The black demons of indifference fled out of their mouths to harden the hearts of these children. So

The Greek expression "in the bosom of Abraham" is shorthand for a position of honor at the banquet of the afterlife. At formal banquets in New Testament times guests would recline on couches instead of sitting on chairs (according to the original Greek, reclining is the consistent posture at the meals of Jesus, as in Mark 2:15; 14:18 and parallels). The positions of the various couches were ranked and diners were placed according to their social status (as in they marched by. None looked Lazarus in the eye.

When all had left, the doors closed and the parking lot emptied, Lazarus looked in his hat. "Fifty cents," said Lazarus to himself, "the veteran's not doing well today."

Lazarus rubbed his stomach, leaned his head against the wall, and closed his eyes.

"Lazarus, Lazarus, wake up," said the short Hispanic woman who now stood beside him.

"Jesus, you scared me! I thought everyone was gone," said Lazarus.

"Oh, Lazarus, you know I wouldn't leave you. But those people, they have hearts of stone," she said.

Lazarus shook his head.

"Come, Lazarus," she said, holding out her hand for him to grasp and haul himself up. She handed him his cane.

"Brunch," she said, and then laughed, "let me take you to brunch."

"Oh, thank you, Jesus, thank you, Jesus," said Lazarus, as he looked down at the white stone building that was receding far, far below. *(Bruce J. Ackerson)*

Luke 14:7-11). To be located "in the bosom" of another diner would simply mean reclining to his right, since diners all reclined on their left elbows and, when sharing a couch, as was common in the Roman triclinium dining room arrangement, reclined side by side diagonal to the table. Reclining just to the right of the patriarch Abraham would then be a position of honor. Thus in the story the situations of the two characters are reversed. Whereas in life the rich man enjoyed fine banquets and Lazarus longed for a mere crumb, in the afterlife Lazarus celebrated at a sumptuous banquet while the rich man longed for a mere drop of water. (Smith, 17, 222, 260)

LUKE 18:1-8

The Persistent Widow

A widow who has been denied justice persistently goes to a judge to demand justice, until the judge finally relents.

The Story

He told them a parable to show that they should keep on praying and never lose heart: 'In a certain city there was a judge who had no fear of God or respect for man, and in the same city there was a widow who kept coming before him to demand justice against her opponent. For a time he refused; but in the end he said to himself, "Although I have no fear of God or respect for man, yet this widow is so great a nuisance that I will give her justice before she wears me out with her persistence."' The Lord said, 'You hear what the unjust judge says. Then will not God give justice to his chosen, to whom he listens patiently while they cry out to him day and night? I tell you, he will give them justice soon enough. But when the Son of Man comes, will he find faith on earth?'

Comments on the Story

In Luke 17:20, the Pharisees ask when the rule of God will come. The listener knows that God's rule is already beginning to be freshly manifest among them through the ministry of Jesus. The church in the book of Acts witnesses to its continuing presence and growth.

Jesus then explains to the disciples that they will long for the apocalyptic cataclysm to bring the rule of God to completion, but it will be delayed (17:21-37). It *will* come with a sudden, violent interruption of present life: similar to a lightning flash, similar to the day Lot left Sodom when fire and sulphur rained from the sky. The disciples must prepare for the advent of God's rule. If they are not prepared, they may be left in a condition similar to Lot's wife, or the woman who was left grinding corn while her companion is taken.

The time of preparation is now, for "Where the carcass is, there will the vultures gather" (17:37). The term "vulture" can also be translated "eagle." The eagle was a symbol of Rome. Only a few years before Luke writes, the Romans sacked Jerusalem and destroyed the temple. A few commentators see this saying as a reference to that event. If so, Luke uses it to alert the community to the fact that they are living in the last days. The rule of God can come at any time.

In Luke 17:20-37, then, Luke simultaneously alerts the community to the prefiguration of the rule of God in the ministry of Jesus and in the ministry of the church. Luke also urges the community to prepare for a delay of the second coming of Jesus (the event that completes the manifestation of the rule of God), and to prepare for the certainty of its arrival—which includes separation and judgment. This multifaceted attitude is consistent with other teachings on the same subject in Luke-Acts (Luke 3:7; 5:35; 8:17; 10:9-11; 11:2; 13:29; 14:17; 21:25-27, 35; Acts 1:11; 2:20; 3:20; 24:25). Jesus emphasizes that those who witness to the coming of the rule of God will suffer (Luke 8:23-27; 21:9-24). The church in Acts suffers just as Jesus said (Acts 4:1-21; 5:17-42; 6:8–8:1; 12:1-11; 16:16-24; 17:1-9; 18:23–19:41; 21:27–28:31).

Plutarch told the following story about how King Philip of Macedon responded to the pleas of a persistent old woman. "When a poor old woman insisted that her case should be heard before him, and often caused him annoyance, he said he had no time to spare, whereupon she burst out, 'Then give up being king.' Philip, amazed at her words, proceeded at once to hear not only her case but those of the others." (*Sayings of Kings and Commanders* 179C-D [late first century C.E.]; from Boring-Berger-Colpe, 230-31, no. 341)

Jesus tells the story of the persistent widow "to show [the disciples] that they should keep on praying and never lose heart." We discovered in connection with the parable of the friend at midnight (Luke 11:1-13) that Christian prayer is fundamentally prayer for the rule of God to come. In prayer, the disciples and the church consciously open themselves to the presence and working of the divine rule, and they ask God to bring that rule to fruition. Given the complicated intellectual and emotional milieu regarding the coming of the divine rule that we sketched in the preceding paragraphs, it is little wonder that some in the Lukan community may have been losing heart.

The setting of the parable is unspecified, "a certain city." Listeners can easily identify their own situation with that of the parable.

The judge neither fears God nor respects human beings. In the ancient world, as today, a judge was charged with seeing that justice was enacted in a community. In the Jewish tradition, justice is a relational notion. The just community is one in which relationships manifest the qualities that God desires; justice particularly includes protection for the vulnerable and marginalized. This judge, however, does not honor God (and consequently God's vision of justice). Similarly, the prophets complain that corrupt judges are present in the covenantal community (Amos 2:6-7; 5:10-13). The Greek verb that is translated "had no . . . respect" can also mean "has no sense of shame."

As is well known, women in the ancient world typically had access to much less power and security than men. In most circumstances, women were dependent upon men, and in certain circumstances women were subject to men. Widows were considered especially vulnerable. Widows had few inheritance rights. Levirate marriage provided widows with some measure of security (Deuteronomy 25:5-10). However, the levirate wife was sometimes accorded secondary status. Some women were left altogether alone, and, therefore, were completely dependent on the compassion of the community for their survival. Since no male is mentioned in connection with our widow, she may be alone in the world.

The Jewish tradition is permeated with divine concern to provide for widows (Exodus 22:21-23; Deuteronomy 10:14-19; 14:29; 16:11, 14; 24:17-22; 26:12-13; 27:19; Jeremiah 49:11). In keeping with the subtheme of judgment present in Luke 17:20-37, the listener also remembers that failure to care for the widows is the cause of the divine judgment (Job 22:9-11; Psalm 94:1-7; Isaiah 1:16-17, 21-25; Malachi 3:5). Later, in the book of Acts, the early church will repeatedly minister to widows in accordance with Jewish prescription (6:1; 9:39, 41).

The injustice suffered by the widow is unspecified. We know only that it involves an "opponent." Someone in the community—perhaps even someone in her family—may have denied her provision. The listener is immensely sympathetic to the widow and confident of God's desire for justice on her behalf. The woman comes to the judge repeatedly and is repeatedly turned away. Her persistence is remarkable, especially if (as we conjecture above) she acts by herself and without benefit of male (or other) systems of support. The woman's persistence authorizes our own protests against injustice.

The judge eventually provides justice for the widow to get rid of her nuisance. In what may be a bit of first-century humor, the phrase that we render "before she wears me out" is more literally "before she gives me a black eye."

Jesus then moves from the lesser to the greater. If a reprobate judge responds to the widow's pleas for injustice in order to get rid of her, how much more will God act on behalf of those who cry to heaven day and night. Indeed, by speaking of God's patience, Jesus invokes one of the deepest and most compassionate divine attributes in the Jewish tradition. The mention of patience also invokes the memory of God's longsuffering with the people (Exodus 34:6; Numbers 14:18; Nehemiah 9:17; Psalms 86:15; 103:8; Wisdom of Solomon 15:1).

God was with the widow in her protracted injustice. So also, God suffers with the church as it awaits the culmination of the divine purposes.

Jesus, the disciples, and the church in Luke-Acts are similar to the widow in that they appear to be relatively weak and vulnerable in comparison to the larger culture in which they live, with its massive social institutions and power. The parable encourages the church to continue to pray for the coming of the divine rule. Prayer in Luke-Acts thus has a double edge. On one side, it opens the community to witness to the divine rule, a witness that sometimes results in suffering. On the other side, prayer itself becomes a means through which God provides for the witnesses in their suffering. For instance, in the garden Jesus asks for the cup to be taken away, but prayer makes it possible for him to go to the cross (Luke 22:39-45). On the cross, in the depths of suffering, Jesus embodies the divine rule by praying for the forgiveness of the executioners (Luke 23:34; see also 6:28). Through prayer, the circle of witnesses is restored to twelve (Acts 1:24) and the community is filled with the Holy Spirit and the boldness to testify (4:31). By means of prayer, the deacons are selected (6:6) to enact justice for the widows (!). Stephen is strengthened in his martyrdom as he prays (Acts 7:59). By means of prayer, the Samaritans receive the Spirit (8:15) and Peter raises the dead (9:40). Peter and Cornelius are brought together through prayer to initiate the Gentile mission (Acts 10:2, 9, 31). When Peter is imprisoned the church prays and God opens the prison doors (12:4-10). Paul and Silas are at prayer when God releases them from prison (16:25). Prayer is a continual part of Paul's final journey (20:36; 21:5; 27:29). This pattern encourages the church in Luke's day to continue its life of prayer in the confidence that prayer helps the church become available for witness and provides for the church in the midst of its witness.

The passage closes with a question that is directed to the listener (Luke 18:8). How can the church maintain its confidence in the coming of the divine realm given its delay, and given the difficulties faced by the Christian community? The preceding story suggests that prayer helps sustain the faith of the disciples and the church until Jesus returns. They need not lose heart. Even if their prayers lead them into dangerous witness, prayer itself will sustain them.

Retelling the Story

> "This widow is so great a nuisance that I will give her justice before she wears me out with her persistence." (Luke 18:5)

The doors to the emergency room rolled open. There was no siren, no paramedics scurrying out of an ambulance, only a medium-sized scruffy-looking woman in a dark winter coat. She brushed the snow off her arms and tucked insulation back into the ripped pocket of her coat.

She walked right up to the receptionist's counter and leaned on it. The receptionist barely looked away from her computer screen and said, "Back again? What is it now?"

The woman pulled up her sleeve to reveal her forearm. "I have this here rash, see," she said.

Picking up the phone the receptionist told her, "You know the routine. Go sit in the waiting room and a nurse will have a look." Then she said into the phone, "Dotty's here."

Behind the closed doors of the emergency room, the doctors and nurses rushed about. The heart attack had just arrived. The overdose was out of danger. But the car accident broken arm awaited attention. The rash would wait.

The new E.R. nurse said, "Dotty, that hypochondriac, again? Isn't this her fourth visit this week? Why doesn't she go to the Doctor's Emergency clinic sometimes?"

Another nurse answered her, "It's private. Doctor's Emergency only takes paying patients. We take the rest. It's craziness, isn't it?"

"Look at this sixty-page medical history," said a third nurse. "It's Dotty's." She clipped the stack of papers to the clipboard. "And here's the list of all her current meds. Having this saves a lot of time. We don't have to get the same old information from her several times a week." The nurse turned and headed toward the waiting room where Dotty sat.

The new E.R. nurse responded, "Great. She demands attention, but doesn't even pay. Some nerve."

"Can't pay," said the second nurse. "Poor Dotty, she has no insurance and can't afford her medications. But she still smokes."

"Smokes?" said the new E.R. nurse. "You know, if she didn't smoke, she would have a lot more money for medications."

The second nurse looked at her and said, "I don't know. She didn't qualify for breast cancer screening. So the cancer was pretty advanced. A double mastectomy. Now chemotherapy. Pretty expensive."

A med tech asked, "Have you seen those cute little flower boxes she makes? She sells them for $20 each, so surely she can pay for some medications."

The emergency room moved at a frenetic pace even when Dotty walked into a patient bay. She sat on the bed waiting to be seen by the doctor. After a few minutes she got up and walked into the next patient bay. The man with the broken arm lay in bed crying. She reached out her dirt-smudged hand and touched him on the arm without the cast.

"What's the matter, Hon? Where do you hurt?"

"I'm broke," said the man. "I have two dollars. And now no car." He sobbed.

"Oh there, there," said Dotty patting his arm. "Two dollars? Why, you can go for a week on two dollars. On Monday you go to the Baptist church for some cash. On Tuesday to the Community Pantry for food. On Wednesday to the Goodwill for clothes. . . ."

"But how do I get there?" the man interrupted. "I have no car."

"Why, my word," said Dotty, "the two dollars—a cab will take you there for two dollars. They understand. You'll be just fine, Hon, just fine. Stick with Dotty."

The new E.R. nurse came into the room and asked, "Dotty, what are you doing in here? You're supposed to be in the next bay . . . and sick."

"It's OK, she's been talking to me. Dotty's been talking to me," said the man.

"Really," said the new E.R. nurse. Dotty pulled the planter out of the paper bag and said to the new nurse, "I have one of these here planters for you, Hon. Only twenty dollars. All your nurse friends have one."

> Ecclesiasticus 35:16-17 teaches that God is a judge who acts fairly in behalf of all: "He has no favourites at the expense of the poor, and he listens to the prayer of the wronged. He never ignores the appeal of the orphan or of the widow as she pours out her complaint."

"Oh, no. Not this time, maybe next time," said the new nurse. "Now you need to move next door."

"Next time, yes, next time," said Dotty with a laugh erupting from the depths of her soul—the deep crackly laughter of a poor, uneducated trickster; a survivor, social worker, and hope-giver. *(Bruce J. Ackerson)*

LUKE 18:9-14

The Pharisee and the Tax Collector

When a Pharisee and a tax collector pray in the temple, Jesus condemns the Pharisee but commends the tax collector.

The Story

Here is another parable that he told; it was aimed at those who were sure of their own goodness and looked down on everyone else. 'Two men went up to the temple to pray, one a Pharisee and the other a tax-collector. The Pharisee stood up and prayed this prayer: "I thank you, God, that I am not like the rest of mankind—greedy, dishonest, adulterous—or, for that matter, like this tax-collector. I fast twice a week; I pay tithes on all that I get." But the other kept his distance and would not even raise his eyes to heaven, but beat upon his breast, saying, "God, have mercy on me, sinner that I am." It was this man, I tell you, and not the other, who went home acquitted of his sins. For everyone who exalts himself will be humbled; and whoever humbles himself will be exalted.'

Comments on the Story

In Luke 17:20, the Pharisees ask a question that reveals their spiritual imperceptivity. As noted in my remarks above on the setting and parable of the persistent widow (Luke 18:1-8), Jesus then urges the disciples to prepare for the apocalyptic cataclysm that will fully manifest the rule of God. When the reign of God comes in its fullness, the unprepared will be left behind. The parable of the persistent widow urges the community to prepare through prayer. The parable of the Pharisee and the tax collector provides the listening community with an example of someone who is not prepared and who will be left behind.

According to 18:9, Jesus aims the parable at those who are "sure of their own goodness and look down on everyone else." The parable is intended to warn Pharisees (and the persons that they represent) so that they can repent of their objections to Jesus and his disciples (and, by extension, the Christian community). These objections focus on the fellowship of Jesus (and, by extension, the church) with tax collectors, sinners, Gentiles, and others who are outside the pale of conventional religious acceptance but whom Luke understands to be embraced in the movement toward the final manifestation of the rule of God. As Luke indicates in a portrayal of the Pharisee Gamaliel, Pharisees need not become Christian in order to support the church's witness (Acts 5:33-39).

Pharisees, as Pharisees, can honor the witness of the church (Acts 22:30–23:11).

The English expression "who were sure of their own goodness" does not call forth the full frame of reference that is implied in the original language. The Greek phrase includes the pivotal term *dikaios*. This term, usually translated more satisfactorily as "righteous" (or less satisfactorily as "justified"), is relational. God is the paradigm of righteousness, for God is "right" within God's own self. God relates to all creatures "rightly" (Psalm 11:7; 19:9; 116:5; 119:137; Wisdom 12:14-15). People are righteous when they live in relationship with God and with one another according to God's design (Psalm 112:1-10; Proverbs 10:1-32; Ecclesiasticus 32:16). In the time of Luke, *dikaios* was often used to refer to relationships in the rule of God (as in 2 Esdras 12:7). When the divine rule comes in its fullness, all people (and all created entities) will relate to one another in the way that God desires. The introduction to the story urges the listeners to consider whether their own understanding and practice of righteousness is of the character required (and created by) the coming of the rule of God.

Interpreters often say that the surprise of the story is the reversal that takes place between the expectation and the evaluation of the two characters. A Pharisaic audience (and others who are sympathetic to them) begins the story assuming that the Pharisee is the exemplar and the tax collector is scum. By the end of the story, their roles are reversed. In this reading, the Pharisaic audience is shocked.

However, the Gospel of Luke consistently portrays the Pharisees negatively (Luke 5:17-26; 6:1-11; 7:24-30, 36-50; 11:37-54; 12:1-3; 14:1-14; 15:1–16:15; 19:29-39). The Lukan Jesus has already exposed the shallowness of the Pharisees' religiosity (esp. 11:37-54) and has even named them hypocrites (12:1-3). On the other hand, Luke pictures Jesus reaching out to the tax collectors,

> The prayer of the Pharisee is viewed negatively in this parable as an example of self-righteousness. However, in traditional Jewish thought, similar prayers of thanksgiving for God's blessings were not viewed as self-righteous but as commendable expressions of piety, such as the following: "I give thanks to Thee, O Lord my God, that Thou has set my portion with those who sit in the Beth ha-Midrash [the house of study] and Thou hast not set my portion with those who sit in [street] corners, for I rise early and they rise early, but I rise early for words of Torah and they rise early for frivolous talk; I labour and they labour, but I labour and receive a reward and they labour and do not receive a reward; I run and they run, but I run to the life of the future world and they run to the pit of destruction." (*b. Berakhot* 28b [ca. sixth century C.E.]; from Scott, 95)

even having table fellowship with them (Luke 5:27-32; 7:24-30; 15:1-32; 19:1-10; see also 3:12). If we have been hearing the Lukan narrative in its unfolding, we are not surprised at Jesus' evaluation of the two characters. The fresh element in the story is the depth of the tax collector's longing to be a part of the rule of God, and the assurance that the tax collector is included in that realm.

In Judaism of antiquity, people typically stood and prayed with eyes open, lifted toward heaven. The Pharisee evidently stands in a place in the temple in which people usually prayed. The Pharisee thanks God for a life that is exemplary in outward respects. By not being greedy (or better: practicing extortion), dishonest, or adulterous, the Pharisee appears to be a moral stalwart in the community. The Pharisee fasts twice a week. Fasting is an act of spiritual discipline, with roots deep in Judaism and with multiple purposes. The hunger of fasting reminds human beings of our complete dependence upon God. It purges the self of concern for peripheral matters and directs us to think about things that are fundamental. It prepares for revelation. Fasting is a means of identification with the hungry (and other needy) of the world and of remembering God's will to provide for them (and of our responsibility to join God in that provision). By tithing, people acknowledge God as the source of their lives, and they commit themselves to live according to God's design. The Pharisee's tithe goes beyond the expectation of Torah (Deuteronomy 14:22-29).

Based only on the description of the Pharisee in the prayer, we would say that the Pharisee is the type of person on whom communities depend for stability and moral direction. However, Luke has already revealed that the Pharisees are, in fact, greedy, dishonest, and adulterous (11:37-41; 16:14-18). The Pharisees tithe, but avoid practicing the covenantal commitments of justice and love that are supposed to be symbolized by the tithe (11:42). Indeed, they burden the people with unnecessary and deceptive practices, and are in league with those who kill the prophets (11:45-52).

The tax collector was disdained by the general Jewish population in the first century. The various levels of government in the ancient world were funded by a tax pyramid. The amount of taxes Caesar needed was to be paid by the next lowest level of government, which then taxed the next lowest level to raise the money. Each level needed to collect enough money to pay for its own operation and to pay the bill to the higher level. The tax collector was responsible for receiving the money from individuals to fund the pyramid. Tax collectors made their own income by collecting more money from the population than the tax collectors themselves owed to the tax pyramid. Tax collectors were free to collect as much money for themselves as they could. Many tax collectors took advantage of their position to take disproportionate amounts for themselves, sometimes inflicting economic hardship on those from whom they extracted taxes. In addition to being disliked for their callous economic exploitation, tax collectors supported the oppressive Roman government. A tax collector in

Judea was typically a Jewish person in the employ of Rome. The tax collector was viewed as a traitor. And tax collectors' dealings with Gentile money often left them unclean. Tax collectors were a threat to God's designs for a righteous community.

The tax collector, evidently feeling a full burden of guilt, does not draw near the ordinary place of prayer but stands at a distance. The revenue agent does not even look toward heaven. With eyes downcast, the tax collector makes an ancient, and emotionally deep, gesture of repentance: the beating of the breast (cf. Luke 23:48). The prayer is simple and heartfelt: "God, have mercy on me, sinner that I am." The same Greek verb for "have mercy" also appears in the Greek translation (Septuagint) of Exodus 32:14 to describe the change of heart when God decides not to destroy Israel after the people made the golden calf. Figuratively speaking, the tax collector has worshiped a golden calf and deserves destruction. But the tax collector trusts that God is merciful, gracious, slow to anger, and abounding in steadfast love (Exodus 34:6).

Why does the tax collector go home righteous rather than the Pharisee? The tax collector repents. The Pharisee does not even recognize the need to repent. The narrative does not explicitly say that the tax collector makes a change of moral behavior, but we can assume such a change. For Luke indicates that repentance results in a lifestyle—including patterns of acquiring and spending money—that embodies the rule of God in community (Luke 3:8-14; 13:1-9; 16:19-31; Acts 2:38–4:37; 8:14-24; 26:19-23). For example, almost immediately Zacchaeus repents by giving half of the superintendent of taxes' estate to the poor (in the spirit of Luke 12:33-34 and 18:22) and by repaying fourfold those who were defrauded in the process of collecting taxes (Luke 19:1-10). The tax collector is transformed from social threat into witness to the divine will for justice.

The final saying (Luke 18:14) is not an incidental appendage. It recollects 9:18-27. The rule of God inverts the usual exercise and order of power. Those who follow the pattern of the old age, and exercise their own power to achieve security, will ultimately be judged. Those who follow Jesus in self-emptying for the sake of the community will discover an immediate community of support (the church as it is described in Acts) and the world that never ends.

In relating to God and the human community, will we be analogous to the distant Pharisee or the repentant, transformed tax collector? As a Christian community, will we learn to embrace the "tax collectors" (outcasts) in our midst who are right with God and who now seek to live rightly in community?

Retelling the Story

> "Everyone who exalts himself will be humbled; and whoever humbles himself will be exalted." (Luke 18:14b)

Noah waited outside the nave doors while the congregation sang the last verse of "The Old Rugged Cross." The preacher walked to the pulpit slowly. He motioned for all to sit as the song ended. In the brief commotion of shuffling feet, Noah slipped through the doors and sat at the very end of the very last pew closest to the door. No one saw him except the preacher, who gave a hard stare. The preacher held his Bible with an outstretched arm and began speaking. "The day is coming, my friends. The day of the Lord is coming," he said, nodding his head.

Noah looked down at his feet and trembled. "Oh God, forgive me."

The preacher opened his Bible and began reading: "Listen to the Word of God in the twentieth chapter of the Revelation. 'And the sea gave up the dead which were in it; and death and hell delivered up the dead which were in them: and they were judged every man according to their works. And death and hell were cast into the lake of fire. This is the second death. And whosoever was not found written in the book of life was cast into the lake of fire.' Is your name in that book? Is your name in the Book of Life?"

Noah saw the congregation nodding in agreement. "Amen, praise God," they said. Noah shook his head and whispered, "God, I am a sinner, have mercy on me."

"A lake of fire. A lake of fire," said the preacher, thumping a finger against the cover of his Bible. "Brothers and sisters, this is no fishing lake. You'd best be here Sunday mornings. Unless you catch your fish deep-fried. If you know what I mean."

Laughter and applause and a chorus of "Amen, brother" filled the room.

The preacher raised his voice and veins showed on his temples. "Hell is a burning lake of fire, a devouring fire. It's the place of the eternally damned. The wicked weep and gnash their teeth. They curse God . . . and cry out for one little drop of water. You don't want to be there."

The preacher raised his arm and pointed his finger at the congregation. "And you don't want to be here for the Tribulation either. If you are, you'll think you've died and gone to Hell. Seven years of Hell on earth. Listen to God's plan for his people from Paul's first letter to the Thessalonians. 'For the Lord himself shall descend from

> Like Jesus, the rabbis also exhorted the pious to be humble: "A favourite saying of the Rabbis of Jabneh was: I am God's creature and my fellow is God's creature. My work is in the town and his work is in the country. I rise early for my work and he rises early for his work. Just as he does not presume to do my work, so I do not presume to do his work. Will you say, I do much and he does little? We have learnt: One may do much or one may do little; it is all one, provided he directs his heart to heaven." (*b. Berakhot* 17a [ca. sixth century C.E.]; from Epstein, 1.101)

heaven with a shout, with the voice of the archangel, and with the trump of God: and the dead in Christ shall rise first. Then we which are alive and remain shall be caught up together with them in the clouds, to meet the Lord in the air: and so shall we ever be with the Lord.' The Rapture. The saved will be carried up to meet Jesus to escape the Tribulation. This is God's plan for the end of the world. It had better be in your plans."

"Amen, praise the Lord," they said. Noah shook his head.

The preacher now shouted, "Are you among the Elect? Or will you be left behind? Will you suffer the Tribulation?"

"Nooo!" said the parishioners. Noah put his head in his hands.

"Choose your friends carefully. Be very careful who you are with, the Rapture comes at an unexpected hour," the preacher continued. "Listen to the second letter of Paul to Timothy: 'This know also, that in the last days perilous times shall come. For men shall be lovers of their own selves, covetous, boasters, proud, blasphemers, disobedient to parents, unthankful, unholy, without natural affection, trucebreakers, false accusers, incontinent, fierce, despisers of those that are good, traitors, heady, high-minded, lovers of pleasures more than lovers of God; having a form of godliness, but denying the power thereof . . . from such turn away.' Avoid them!" said the preacher. Noah slowly rose to his feet and, with his head hanging low, slipped out the door. The fiery anger on the preacher's face dissolved to a smile.

A week later Noah walked to the twenty-four-hour corner store for a few groceries. As he walked home he stopped at a T-shirt lying on the ground. It looked new. He walked around it trying to read what it said. Finally he leaned down and picked it up. He held it up with one hand and read to himself, "Rapture Ready." "Creepy, just like the T-shirts people wore in that church," he thought. "Oh my gosh. It couldn't be." He walked more quickly toward his apartment. "Is it quieter than usual?" he asked himself. There was an empty car straddling a fire hydrant. People stood around. Water sprayed out from under the car. The bumper sticker on the car said, "Beware, in case of the Rapture, this car will be driverless." Noah began running with the grocery bag clutched to his chest. He ran past his apartment to the church. He ran inside. There sat half a dozen people scattered about the nave. They looked stunned, except for the homeless man sleeping on one of the pews. An older gray-haired woman turned to him and said, "Oh my God, now the Tribulation."

Noah said, "I haven't been to church since I was a child, except last . . . Oh, I don't know what to do. What can we do?"

"Nothing," said the gray-haired woman. "We can do nothing. It is out of our hands. It is God's plan for the future." She looked stone-faced and then shrieked, "Are they really gone? I want to hear them singing. Please, God."

Noah moved to sit beside her and touched her hand with his. Then he sang in a frail, hesitating voice, "Jesus loves me this I know . . ."

The gray-haired woman joined in: ". . . for the Bible tells me so, little ones whom he adores, they are weak but He is strong."

The others slowly got up and moved toward them singing, "Yes, Jesus loves me. Yes, Jesus loves me. Yes, Jesus loves me. The Bible tells me so." They stood together in a small circle now and sang the song again.

Noah saw the homeless man staring at his grocery bag. He hesitated, then said, "I have a few groceries I can share with you."

"I sure could use something to eat. Been a long time," the homeless man said. Noah opened his loaf of bread and handed the homeless man a slice.

"The Body of Christ," said the gray-haired woman, holding out her hands. Noah handed her a slice of bread. "The Body of Christ," they repeated in unison. Noah continued handing each person a slice of bread. They ate. Then Noah invited them to sit on the floor and share the remaining groceries. *(Bruce J. Ackerson)*

Selected Bibliography

References in the text are cited by author.

Boring, M. Eugene, Klaus Berger, and Carsten Colpe, eds. *Hellenistic Commentary to the New Testament.* Nashville: Abingdon Press, 1995.

Braude, William G. *The Midrash on Psalms.* 2 volumes. New Haven: Yale University Press, 1959.

———. *Pesikta rabbati; discourses for feasts, fasts, and special Sabbaths.* 2 volumes. New Haven: Yale University Press, 1968.

Charles, R. H. *Apocrypha and Pseudepigrapha of the Old Testament.* 2 volumes. Oxford: Clarendon Press, 1913.

Epstein, Isidore. *The Babylonian Talmud.* 34 volumes. London: Soncino Press, 1935-48.

Freedman, Harry, ed. *Midrash Rabbah.* 13 volumes. London: Soncino Press, 1939.

Goldin, Judah. *The Fathers According to Rabbi Nathan.* New Haven: Yale University Press, 1955.

Hammer, Reuven. *Sifre: A Tannaitic Commentary on the Book of Deuteronomy.* New Haven: Yale University Press, 1986.

Philo. *Supplement II: Questions and Answers on Exodus.* Trans. Ralph Marcus. Loeb Classical Library. Cambridge: Harvard University Press, 1970.

Scott, Bernard Brandon. *Hear Then the Parable: A Commentary on the Parables of Jesus.* Minneapolis: Fortress Press, 1989.

Smith, Dennis E. *From Symposium to Eucharist: The Banquet in the Early Christian World.* Minneapolis: Fortress Press, 2003.

Young, Brad H. *Jesus and His Jewish Parables: Rediscovering the Roots of Jesus' Teaching.* New York: Paulist Press, 1989.

Index of Readings from *The Revised Common Lectionary*

Index of Parallel Stories

ANCIENT NEAR EASTERN

OLD TESTAMENT APOCRYPHA AND PSEUDEPIGRAPHA

RABBINIC LITERATURE

OTHER JEWISH LITERATURE

EARLY CHRISTIAN LITERATURE

GREEK AND ROMAN LITERATURE

PAPYRI